THiNK

WORKBOOK 2

Herbert Puchta, Jeff Stranks & Peter Lewis-Jones

B1

T0349635

CAMBRIDGE
UNIVERSITY PRESS

Acknowledgements

The authors and publishers acknowledge the following sources of copyright material and are grateful for the permissions granted. While every effort has been made, it has not always been possible to identify the sources of all the material used, or to trace all copyright holders. If any omissions are brought to our notice, we will be happy to include the appropriate acknowledgements on reprinting.

The Zoological Society of London for the text on p. 61 from the London Zoo website. Reproduced with permission;

The Guardian for the text on p. 63 adapted from 'Experience: I became a pop star overnight. The next morning I found out my song had gone to number one, beating Lady Gaga, Justin Bieber and Katy Perry' by Kashy Keegan, *The Guardian*, 15/03/2014. Copyright ©Guardian News & Media Ltd 2014;

Daily Mail for the text on p. 94 adapted from 'Bandy-legged Belle the "spider dog" runs for the first time thanks to £3,000 operation', *Daily Mail* 29/07/2010. Copyright © Daily Mail, 2010;

ABC News Video Source for the text on p. 99 adapted from '7 Simple Ways to Stay Healthier at Work' by Enjoli Francis and Kim Carollo, 11/0`8/2011. www.abcnews.go.com. Reproduced with permission.

Corpus
Development of this publication has made use of the Cambridge English Corpus (CEC). The CEC is a computer database of contemporary spoken and written English, which currently stands at over one billion words. It includes British English, American English and other varieties of English. It also includes the Cambridge Learner Corpus, developed in collaboration with Cambridge English Language Assessment. Cambridge University Press has built up the CEC to provide evidence about language use that helps to produce better language teaching materials.

English Profile
This product is informed by the English Vocabulary Profile, built as part of English Profile, a collaborative programme designed to enhance the learning, teaching and assessment of English worldwide. Its main funding partners are Cambridge University Press and Cambridge English Language Assessment and its aim is to create a 'profile' for English linked to the Common European Framework of Reference for Languages (CEF). English Profile outcomes, such as the English Vocabulary Profile, will provide detailed information about the language that learners can be expected to demonstrate at each CEF level, offering a clear benchmark for learners' proficiency. For more information, please visit www.englishprofile.org

Cambridge Dictionaries
Cambridge dictionaries are the world's most widely used dictionaries for learners of English. The dictionaries are available in print and online at dictionary.cambridge.org. Copyright © Cambridge University Press, reproduced with permission.

The publishers are grateful to the following for permission to reproduce copyright photographs and material:

T = Top, B = Below, L = Left, R = Right, C = Centre, B/G = Background

p. 5: ©sumnersgraphicsinc/iStock/360/Getty Images; p. 14 (T): ©George C. Beresford /Hulton Archive/Getty Images; p. 14 (B): ©Pictorial Parade /Archive Photos/Getty Images; p. 16: ©BEI/Gregory Pace/REX; p. 19: ©bikeriderlondon/ Shutterstock; p. 20: ©Lightspring/Shutterstock; p. 21 (0): ©Krasimira Nevenova/ Shutterstock; p. 21 (1): ©Björn Höglund/Alamy; p. 21 (2): ©moodboard/360/ Getty Images; p. 21 (3): ©Elnur/Shutterstock; p. 21 (4): ©belchonock/iStock/360/ Getty Images; p. 21 (5): ©Paul Fleet/iStock/360/Getty Images; p. 21 (6): ©MOT-Foto/iStock/360/Getty Images; p. 21 (7): ©greenleaf123/iStock/360/Getty Images; p. 22: ©Ashwin Kharidehal Abhirama/iStock/360/Getty Images; p.22 (B/G): ©blue67design/Shutterstock; p. 24 (TL): ©DWaschnig/Shutterstock; p. 24 (TR): ©Karkas/Shutterstock; p. 24 (BL): ©Ron Ellis/Shutterstock; p. 24 (BR): ©ACE STOCK LIMITED/Alamy; p. 33: ©Siri Stafford/Digital Vision; p. 34 (TL): ©trappy76/iStock/360/Getty Images; p. 34 (TR dvd and box): ©Henry Leib/ iStock/360/Getty Images; p. 34 (TR dancer): ©R. Gino Santa Maria/Shutterstock; p. 34 (BL): ©GeorgeMPhotography/Shutterstock; p. 34 (BR): ©Minerva Studio/ iStock/360/Getty Images; p. 45: ©INTERFOTO/Alamy; p. 48 (TL): ©Stockbyte/ Getty Images; p. 48 (TCL): ©Balefire/Shutterstock; p. 48 (TCR): ©serji_o/ iStock/360/Getty Images; p. 48 (TR): ©Stockbyte/Getty Images; p. 48 (BL): ©VvoeVale/iStock/360/Getty Images; p. 48 (BCL): ©Hemera Technologies/ PhotoObjects.net/360/Getty Images; p. 48 (BCR): ©Hemera Technologies/ PhotoObjects.net/360/Getty Images; p. 48 (BR): ©Stockbyte/Getty Images; p. 50: ©AGF s.r.l./REX; p. 51: ©MediaPunch/REX; p. 53: ©Kalenik Hanna/Shutterstock; p. 57 (T): ©rusty13599/iStock/360/Getty Images; p. 57 (C): ©SlobodanMiljevic/ iStock/360/Getty Images; p. 57 (B): ©Justin Kase zfivez / Alamy; p. 58: ©*/Kyodo/ Newscom; p. 61: ©Dan Kitwood /Getty Images Sport/Getty Images; p. 63: ©M & Y News Ltd/REX; p. 68: ©godrick/Shutterstock; p. 76: UNIVERSAL/THE KOBAL COLLECTION; p. 77 (tablets): ©keith morris/Alamy; p. 77 (aeroplane): ©Arena Photo UK/Shutterstock; p. 77 (car): ©Andrey Burmakin/Shutterstock; p. 77 (lift): ©KieferPix/Shutterstock; p. 77 (syringe): ©Ensuper/Shutterstock; p. 77 (wheel): ©Jomar Aplaon/Shutterstock; p. 81: ©PARAMOUNT/THE KOBAL COLLECTION; p. 85 (TR): ©Philippe TURPIN/Photononstop/Corbis; p. 85 (L): ©Horizons WWP/Alamy; p. 85 (BR): ©Valua Vitaly/Shutterstock; p. 87 (L): ©Dimitry Bobroff/Alamy; p. 87 (R): ©joyfuldesigns/Shutterstock; p. 92 (TL): ©Aleksandr Markin/Shutterstock; p. 92 (TC): ©Cathy Yeulet/Hemera/360/ Getty Images; p. 92 (TR): ©James Steidl/Shutterstock; p. 92 (BL): ©Lisa F. Young/ iStock/360/Getty Images; p. 92 (BC): ©Monkey Business Images/Shutterstock; p. 92 (BR): ©Jinga/Shutterstock; p. 94: ©SWNS; p. 104: ©Jon Furniss /WireImage/ Getty Images; p. 105: ©Xavier Vila/age fotostock/Getty Images; p. 112: ©thislife pictures/Alamy; p. 113 (L): ©Lorelyn Medina/Shutterstock; p. 113 (R): ©Kevin Dodge/Corbis; p. 115: ©JLImages/Alamy; p. 117 (T): ©Rashad Penn/ Shutterstock; p. 117 (B): ©anekoho/Shutterstock.

Cover photographs by: (TL): ©Tim Gainey/Alamy; (C): ©hugh sturrock/Alamy; (R): ©Andrea Haase/iStock/Getty Images Plus, Getty Images; (BL): ©Oliver Burston/Alamy.

The publishers are grateful to the following illustrators:
David Semple 5, 8, 15, 34, 40, 46, 60, 66, 73, 75, 80, 90, 108;
Julian Mosedale 4, 10, 29, 37, 42, 54, 64, 72, 74, 78, 86, 95, 114

The publishers are grateful to the following contributors:
Blooberry: text design and layouts; Claire Parson: cover design; Hilary Fletcher: picture research; Leon Chambers: audio recordings; Karen Elliott: Pronunciation sections; Matt Norton: Get it right! exercises

CONTENTS

Welcome   4

UNIT 1 Amazing People   10

Grammar	10
Vocabulary	12
Reading	14
Writing	15
Listening	16
Exam practice: Preliminary	17

UNIT 2 The Ways We Learn   18

Grammar	18
Vocabulary	20
Reading	22
Writing	23
Listening	24
Exam practice: Preliminary	25
Consolidation 1 & 2	**26**

UNIT 3 That's Entertainment   28

Grammar	28
Vocabulary	30
Reading	32
Writing	33
Listening	34
Exam practice: Preliminary	35

UNIT 4 Social Networking   36

Grammar	36
Vocabulary	38
Reading	40
Writing	41
Listening	42
Exam practice: Preliminary	43
Consolidation 3 & 4	**44**

UNIT 5 My Life in Music   46

Grammar	46
Vocabulary	48
Reading	50
Writing	51
Listening	52
Exam practice: Preliminary	53

UNIT 6 Making a Difference   54

Grammar	54
Vocabulary	56
Reading	58
Writing	59
Listening	60
Exam practice: Preliminary	61
Consolidation 5 & 6	**62**

UNIT 7 Future Fun   64

Grammar	64
Vocabulary	66
Reading	68
Writing	69
Listening	70
Exam practice: Preliminary	71

UNIT 8 Science Counts   72

Grammar	72
Vocabulary	74
Reading	76
Writing	77
Listening	78
Exam practice: Preliminary	79
Consolidation 7 & 8	**80**

UNIT 9 What a Job!   82

Grammar	82
Vocabulary	84
Reading	86
Writing	87
Listening	88
Exam practice: Preliminary	89

UNIT 10 Keep Healthy   90

Grammar	90
Vocabulary	92
Reading	94
Writing	95
Listening	96
Exam practice: Preliminary	97
Consolidation 9 & 10	**98**

UNIT 11 Making the News   100

Grammar	100
Vocabulary	102
Reading	104
Writing	105
Listening	106
Exam practice: Preliminary	107

UNIT 12 Playing by the Rules   108

Grammar	108
Vocabulary	110
Reading	112
Writing	113
Listening	114
Exam practice: Preliminary	115
Consolidation 11 & 12	**116**

Pronunciation   page 118   **Grammar reference**   page 122   **Irregular verb list**   page 128

WELCOME

A GETTING TO KNOW YOU
Asking questions

1 Put the words in order to make questions.

0 are / from / where / you

Where are you from _____ ?

1 you / 15 / are

_____ ?

2 doing / you / are / what

_____ ?

3 do / do / you / what

_____ ?

4 do / like / doing / you / what

_____ ?

5 like / you / TV / watching / do

_____ ?

2 Write the questions.

0 A *Are you 13* _____ ?

B Yes, I am. Last Saturday was my 13th birthday.

1 A _____ ?

B I'm just finishing my homework. I won't be long.

2 A _____ ?

B India, but I live in the UK.

3 A _____ ?

B Yes, I do, especially football.

4 A _____ ?

B Hanging out with my friends. That's my favourite thing.

5 A _____ ?

B I'm a teacher.

3 Answer the questions in Exercise 2 so that they are true for you.

_____

_____

_____

_____

_____

The weather

1 Match the pictures and the sentences.

0 It's dry and cloudy. `F`

1 It's warm and sunny. ☐

2 It's cold and foggy. ☐

3 It's hot and humid. ☐

4 It's wet and windy. ☐

5 It's rainy and freezing. ☐

Families

1 Complete the sentences. Use the words in the list.

~~wife~~ | granddad | father | cousin | mother
husband | sister | grandma | aunt | uncle

0 My mother is my father's ___*wife*___ .

1 My _____ is my mother's mother.

2 My _____ is my aunt's child.

3 My uncle is my aunt's _____ .

4 My aunt is my cousin's _____ .

5 My aunt is my father's _____ .

6 My _____ is my grandmother's husband.

7 My _____ is my cousin's father.

8 My _____ is my mother's husband.

9 My mother's sister is my _____ .

2 🔊 02 **Listen and complete the table.**

	Relation to Zoë	Age	Nationality	Job
Jess				student
Tom				
Karen				

3 **Choose three people from your family. Write one or two sentences about each one.**

My aunt's name is Laura. She's from Brasilia.

She's 34 and she's a businesswoman.

_____

_____

_____

SUMMING UP

1 Circle **the correct words.**

A Hey, what ⁰*you are / are you* doing?

B I'm writing an email to my ¹*cousin / sister* Gabriel in Buenos Aires.

A In Buenos Aires? What ²*does he do / is he doing* there? Is he there on holiday?

B Yes. His mother – my ³*aunt / uncle* – married an Argentinian man. They're there on holiday, visiting the family.

A That's nice. Is the weather good there right now?

B Yes, Gabriel said it was ⁴*hot and sunny / freezing.*

A Hot? But it's January!

B In Argentina, January is summer, remember?

A Oh, right. Listen. ⁵*Are you / Do you* like watching films on TV?

B Yes, why?

A There's a great film on this evening. Come and watch it with us.

B OK, thanks. But I'll finish my email first!

B EXPERIENCES
Meeting people (tense revision)

1 **Match the pictures and the sentences.**

1 She's met lots of famous people. ☐

2 She met the president last night. ☐

3 She was having dinner with the president when her phone rang. ☐

2 **Complete the sentences. Use *he* and the verb *eat* in the tenses in brackets.**

0 _He ate_ a really good curry last night. (past simple positive)

1 _____ any breakfast this morning. (past simple negative)

2 A _____ all his vegetables? (past simple question)

B _____ (negative short answer)

3 _____ when I phoned him. (past continuous statement)

4 A _____ Japanese food? (present perfect question with *ever*)

B _____ (positive short answer)

3 **Complete the sentences. Use the correct forms of the verbs.**

A Have you ever ⁰_been_ (be) late for a concert?

B Yes. I ¹_____ (be) late for a big concert last year. It was Florence and the Machine.

A What ²_____ (happen)?

B Well, I ³_____ (miss) my train. So I ⁴_____ (get) to the concert hall at 9 o'clock, not 8 o'clock.

A ⁵_____ you _____ (see) the show?

B Yes. The concert ⁶_____ (start) at 8.45, so of course, when I ⁷_____ (go) in the band ⁸_____ (play). But I ⁹_____ (see) about 75 per cent of the show. And it's the best concert I ¹⁰_____ ever _____ (see)!

Irregular past participles

1 **Write the past participles of the verbs.**

1 think _____ 6 go _____

2 ride _____ 7 see _____

3 have _____ 8 win _____

4 drink _____ 9 eat _____

5 read _____ 10 wear _____

2 Complete the sentences. Use the verbs from Exercise 1.

0 Someone has _drunk_ my orange juice!

1 This book's great. I've _____ it five times.

2 I haven't _____ the film yet. Is it good?

3 I love motorbikes, but I've never _____ one.

4 I've got a suit, but I've never _____ it.

5 She isn't here. She's _____ to the park.

6 I've never _____ a prize.

3 Complete the sentences. Use the correct forms of the verbs.

0 No ice cream, thanks. I've _eaten_ (eat) enough.

1 Oh, you're from Peru? I _____ (think) you were Spanish.

2 This book is great. Have you _____ (read) it?

3 I've _____ (lose) my keys. Have you got them?

4 We _____ (run), but we still missed the train.

5 I _____ (go) to bed late, so I'm tired today.

6 I know I've _____ (see) that man before, but I can't remember where it was.

7 I _____ (wear) this dress to the party last week.

8 We _____ (ride) 30 km on our bikes yesterday.

Losing things

1 Put the conversation in order.

☐ JACK What did you lose?

☐ JACK So what did you do? Did you find it?

☐ JACK What?! That's not losing something – that's just a story about being untidy!

[1] JACK Have you ever lost anything really important?

☐ JACK How did you find it? Where was it?

☐ JACK That's terrible! How did you feel?

☐ DANA My mobile phone. It wasn't expensive, but it had all my friends' numbers on it.

☐ DANA Well, I got my mum's phone and I rang my number. I heard it ringing. It was somewhere in my bedroom. I looked in the wardrobe. It wasn't there. Then I looked under the bed and there it was.

☐ DANA Horrible. It was like losing my whole life.

☐ DANA Yes, I have.

☐ DANA Yes, happily, I did.

2 Read the conversation again. Answer the questions.

0 What did Dana lose?
She lost her mobile phone.

1 How did she feel about losing it?
_____

2 Why did she feel this way?
_____

3 How did she find it?
_____

4 Where did she find it?
_____

5 What does Jack think about her story?
_____

Furniture

1 Put the words in order to make items in a house.

0 keds _desk_

1 elvsesh _____

2 pretac _____

3 reshwo _____

4 otilte _____

5 oreokc _____

6 foas _____

7 rirrmo _____

8 archmira _____

9 bedrarow _____

10 nustaric _____

11 palm _____

2 Which of the items in Exercise 1 might you find in each room? Some items might be in more than one room.

1 bedroom
wardrobe

2 living room
_____

3 kitchen
_____

4 dining room
_____

5 bathroom
_____

SUMMING UP

1 (Circle) the correct words.

A   Why didn't you come to the match yesterday?

B   Oh, I was busy. I ⁰*painted* / (*was painting*) my bedroom. I still ¹*haven't finished* / *didn't finish*.

A   Are you just changing the colour of the walls?

B   No, I've got some new things, too. Last weekend I ²*bought* / *have bought* a new desk and some ³*shelves* / *curtains* for the window. I want to get a new lamp, too. But I ⁴*didn't see* / *haven't seen* anything I like yet.

A   There's a new shop in town. I saw it when we ⁵*shopped* / *were shopping*. They've got nice lamps.

B   Thanks. I'll go and have a look.

C   EATING AND DRINKING
Buying and talking about food

1   Complete the questions using the words in the list.

~~got any~~ | everything | How many | else
How much | Would you like | help you

0   Have you _____got any_____ of those Spanish oranges?

1   Is that _____?

2   Can I _____?

3   _____ would you like?

4   _____ some of those?

5   Anything _____?

6   _____ is that?

2   🔊03   Complete the conversation with the phrases from Exercise 1. Then listen and check.

ASSISTANT   Good afternoon. ⁰ _Can I help you?_

CUSTOMER   Yes, I'd like some apples, please.

ASSISTANT   ¹_____

CUSTOMER   Six big ones, please.

ASSISTANT   OK, ²_____

CUSTOMER   Yes. ³_____

ASSISTANT   I'm afraid we haven't got any. We've got some really nice ones from South Africa.
⁴_____

CUSTOMER   Sure. I'll have three.

ASSISTANT   ⁵_____

CUSTOMER   Yes, it is. ⁶_____

ASSISTANT   That's £3.80 altogether.

CUSTOMER   Here you are.

ASSISTANT   And £1.20 change. Thanks!

3 (Circle) the correct words.

0   I think there are (*some*) / *any* eggs in the fridge.

1   I don't want *some* / *any* cake, thanks.

2   I'd like 500 grams of cheese and *some* / *any* ham, please.

3   I'm sorry. There isn't *some* / *any* pizza left.

4   I haven't got *some* / *any* butter in my sandwich.

5   This soup is really good. Try *some* / *any*.

In a restaurant

1   Put the words in order to make sentences. Write W (waiter) or C (customer).

0   I / the / please / can / menu, / see   ☐ C
_Can I see the menu, please_____ ?

1   ready / you / are / order / to   ☐
_____ ?

2   OK / everything / is   ☐
_____ ?

3   much / too / chicken / the / salt / on / there's   ☐
_____ .

4   can / please / have / bill, / the / we   ☐
_____ ?

5   a / please / four, / for / table   ☐
_____ .

2   Complete the sentences with *much* or *many*.

0   There are too _____many_____ small children in this restaurant.

1   There is too _____ salt in this soup.

2   There are too _____ things on the menu.

3   There's too _____ noise in here.

4   There are too _____ chairs at this table.

5   That's too _____ money.

3   Match the sentences from Exercise 2 with the replies.

a   I agree. It's disgusting.   ☐

b   I'll take some away. How many do you need?   ☐

c   Yes, I really don't know what to choose.   ☐

d   That's no problem. It's your birthday and I want you to choose whatever you want.   ☐

e   Well, it is a family restaurant.   ☐ 0

f   Yes, let's go somewhere quieter.   ☐

Shops / Things you have to do

1 Look at the pictures. Write the shops.

chemist's _____   _____

_____   _____

2 (Circle) the correct words. Then match the sentences with the pictures from Exercise 1.

a You _have to / don't have to_ put a stamp on it. ☐ `3`

b You _have to / don't have to_ wait here. ☐

c You _have to / don't have to_ try clothes on over there. ☐

d You _have to / don't have to_ keep medicines away from children. ☐

3 What do these customer notices mean? Write sentences using _have to_ or _don't have to_.

0 'Buy now, pay later.'
   You can have the item now, but you don't have to pay for it yet.

1 'Please ask assistant before trying on clothes.'
   _____

2 'Cash only – no credit or debit cards accepted.'
   _____

3 'We can deliver your shopping to your home.'
   _____

SUMMING UP

1 Complete the conversations. Write one word in each space.

0 A Why are you going to the _newsagent's_ ?
   B To buy a magazine.

1 A My pen's broken.
   B Well, you don't _____ to buy a new one. You can use mine.

2 A I'd like _____ olives, please. 250 grams.
   B OK, here you are. Anything _____ ?

3 A What's the matter?
   B I don't feel well. I've eaten too _____ food.

D LOOKING AHEAD
Plans and arrangements

1 Look at Mia's diary. Write her plans for the day.

TODAY
8 am – meet Liam for breakfast
10 am – walk in park with Olivia
1 pm – lunch with Mum and Dad
3 pm – dentist
6 pm – train to Manchester
9 pm – film with Paula

0 At 8 am _she's meeting Liam for breakfast._

1 After that _____

2 At 1 pm _____

3 Two hours later _____

4 At 6 pm _____

5 Finally, at 9 pm _____

2 Read the sentences and write _I_ (intention) or _A_ (arrangement).

0 We're having a coffee too. ☐ `A`

1 I'm going to read during the journey. ☐

2 I'm going to have yogurt and cereal. ☐

3 We're meeting at the new restaurant in town. ☐

4 I'm just having a check-up – I hope. ☐

5 We're seeing Jennifer Lawrence's latest film – I can't wait. ☐

3 Write about four arrangements you've got for this week.

_____
_____
_____
_____

Sports and sport verbs

1 (Circle) the correct words.

0 Do you want to _go / do / (play)_ football later?

1 We _went / did / played_ skiing last weekend.

2 My friend Alex _goes / does / plays_ rock climbing every weekend.

3 We have to _go / do / play_ gymnastics on Fridays.

4 I hate tennis. I never want to _go / do / play_ it again!

5 Mum _goes / does / plays_ running every morning.

6 We go to the sports ground on Sundays to _go / do / play_ some athletics.

7 Let's go to the gym. We can _go / do / play_ karate.

Travel and plans

1 Match the sentence halves.

0 We arrived late at the railway station and missed   **f**

1 It was late and we were tired, so we took ☐

2 My mum's car is at the garage, so I rode ☐

3 We left the cinema at 10 pm and caught ☐

4 Last year we flew ☐

5 He really wanted to get home, so he drove ☐

a my bike to school today.

b the last bus home.

c to Colombia for our holidays.

d a taxi home from the airport.

e all night.

f the train by three minutes.

2 Write five sentences about the transport you use in your life.

0 *When we go on holiday, we usually fly.*

1 _____

2 _____

3 _____

4 _____

5 _____

3 🔊04 **Listen to the conversation. Answer the questions.**

0 Where is Martha going for her holiday?
She's going to Italy.

1 How long is she going for?
_____

2 How is she getting there?
_____

3 When is she leaving?
_____

4 What does she need to buy in town?
_____

5 What's her problem?
_____

4 🔊04 **Complete the conversation with the words in the list. Then listen again and check.**

~~going to have~~ | going to be | going to buy
taking | taxi | driving | leaving | flying
going to spend | train

BEN   Are you ⁰ *going to have* a holiday this year?

MARTHA   Yes. We're ¹_____ two weeks in Italy.

BEN   Lucky you. Are you ²_____?

MARTHA   No, we're not. We're ³_____ the train. It's ⁴_____ a real adventure.

BEN   That sounds really exciting.

MARTHA   Yes, in fact, we're ⁵_____ next Monday. We're taking a ⁶_____ to the station and then it's the ⁷_____ all the way to Genoa.

BEN   Are you ready to go?

MARTHA   Almost. I'm ⁸_____ to town tomorrow to do a few last-minute things.

BEN   Like what?

MARTHA   Well, I'm ⁹_____ some more summer clothes and then I need to go to the post office.

BEN   The post office? Why?

MARTHA   I've got to get a new passport.

BEN   A passport! You can't just get a passport that quickly.

MARTHA   Oh. Can't you?

SUMMING UP

1 Complete the email. Write one word in each space.

Hi Jack,

You know our school volleyball team won the local championship last year, right? Well, this month we're playing teams from other cities in the UK.

Next Saturday, we're ⁰ *playing* against a team in Scotland. It's a long way, so we aren't ¹_____ the train – we're ²_____ there! I've never been on a plane before, so I'm really excited.

I'm going to stay in Scotland until Monday. On Sunday, I hope to ³_____ some rock climbing. There are some great places for it up there. My friend Steve wants to ⁴_____ skiing, but I don't think there's enough snow.

I'll write when we come back and tell you all about it.
Best,
Sandy

1 | AMAZING PEOPLE

GRAMMAR

Present perfect with *just*, *already* and *yet* `SB p.14`

1 ★☆☆ Complete the sentences with *just*, *already* or *yet*.

My little sister is really smart.

1 She's _____ learned to walk. She took her first steps last week.

2 She hasn't learned to read _____ , but she likes the pictures.

3 She's _____ learned to count from one to five and she's only one year old!

2 ★★☆ Look at Jake's to-do list for tidying his bedroom. Write sentences using *already* and *yet*.

- tidy desk ✓
- put CDs on shelf ✗
- pick up towels and put them in bathroom ✗
- make bed ✓
- take bin downstairs ✗
- hang up clothes ✓

Jake has *already tidied his desk.*

_____

_____

Jake hasn't _____

_____

_____

3 ★★★ Look at the pictures. What has just happened? Write sentences using the verbs in A and the words in B.

A	B
~~wake~~	~~up~~
fall	a goal
have	an accident
score	over
start	the trophy
win	to rain

0 He *has just woken up.*

1 They _____

2 They _____

3 She _____

4 She _____

5 It _____

Present perfect vs. past simple `SB p.17`

4 ★☆☆ **Match the questions and answers.**

0 | b | Have you played volleyball?
1 | ☐ | Where did you play?
2 | ☐ | Did you enjoy it?
3 | ☐ | Were you good at it?
4 | ☐ | Has your team won anything?
5 | ☐ | Has your team been to different countries?

a No, I wasn't.
b Yes, I have.
c Yes, we've already won three competitions.
d At school.
e No, we haven't – not yet.
f No, not very much.

5 ★★☆ **Complete the conversation. Use the present perfect or past simple and the information in brackets.**

It's Sunday afternoon.

PETER Mum, I'm bored. What can I do?

MUM (finish your homework?)
⁰ *Have you finished your homework?*

PETER (last night)
Yes, I finished it all last night.

MUM (tidy your room?)
1 _____

PETER (yesterday)
2 _____

MUM (take the dog out?)
3 _____

PETER (before lunch)
4 _____

MUM (wash your bike?)
5 _____

PETER (on Friday)
6 _____

MUM (phone Jim?)
7 _____

PETER (this morning / no answer)
8 _____

MUM (watch your new DVD?)
9 _____

PETER (last night)
10 _____

MUM Well, I don't know. What about helping me with the washing up?

PETER Erm … maybe not!

6 ★★★ **Complete the text. Use the present perfect or past simple of the verbs in the list. You can use some verbs more than once.**

do | have | work | not finish | not learn
stop | be | buy | live | get | look

My grandmother is 65 and ⁰*has done* a lot of things in her life. She ¹_____ born in the country and ²_____ on a small farm until she was sixteen. She ³_____ in many different places, but she always says the farm ⁴_____ the best place of all. She ⁵_____ school because she started working when she was fifteen. She ⁶_____ many different jobs in her life – she ⁷_____ a children's nurse, a dressmaker and a shop assistant among other things. She ⁸_____ in a very expensive shop in London for several years. She ⁹_____ working after she ¹⁰_____ married. She ¹¹_____ five children and she ¹²_____ after the house. Grandma loves new things. She ¹³_____ just _____ a laptop, but she ¹⁴_____ how to send emails yet. I'm going to her house to help her now.

GET IT RIGHT!
Present perfect with *just*, *already* and *yet*

Learners often make word order errors with *just*, *already* and *yet*.

✓ I **have just** finished my homework.
✗ I ~~just have~~ finished my homework.

✓ He has not **passed his exam yet**.
✗ He has not ~~passed yet his exam~~.

✓ We **have already finished** our project.
✗ We ~~already have finished~~ our project.

Correct the following sentences.

0 I already have finished my application.
I have already finished my application.

1 My brother has yet not had a summer job.
_____

2 I already have learned to drive.
_____

3 My friends and I have been just on holiday.
_____

4 Have you yet bought your mum a birthday present?
_____

5 The singer has released already five albums.
_____

6 I just have finished writing my blog for this week.
_____

VOCABULARY

Personality adjectives

positive · serious · talented · active · brave · caring · charming · cheerful · confident · cool · creative · easy-going · famous · friendly · funny · intelligent · laid-back · popular

Collocations

do a degree / an interview
make a cake / friends
miss the bus / your family
sign a contract / an autograph
win a competition / a prize
write a novel / a song

just

It was **just** a joke.
Tom's **just** arrived.
The book was **just** fantastic!

Key words in context

admire	She never gives up, and I **admire** her for that.
attract	The Eiffel Tower **attracts** thousands of visitors every year.
complain	The food was horrible, so we decided to **complain** to the waiter.
decorate	I'm going to **decorate** my bedroom with pictures and posters.
genius	He wrote music when he was only five years old! He was a **genius**.
hero	She helped the country to become independent, and now she's a national **hero**.
organise	I'm going to **organise** a party for him.
original	No one else paints like him – he has very **original** ideas.
poem	I gave her a book of **poems** for her birthday.
round of applause	The audience loved the music, and they gave the musicians a big **round of applause** at the end.

Personality adjectives `SB p.12`

1 ★★☆ (Circle) the correct option: A, B or C.

0	An active person	A loves theatre.	(B) is always doing something.	C sleeps a lot.
1	A brave person	A takes risks when it's necessary.	B is often angry.	C doesn't like talking.
2	A creative person	A often makes mistakes.	B has original ideas.	C works very hard.
3	A charming person	A is very good-looking.	B has a lot of money.	C is easy to talk to.
4	A cheerful person	A often feels sad.	B enjoys life.	C often gets angry.
5	A laid-back person	A is very relaxed.	B can't wake up in the morning.	C never goes out.
6	A confident person	A doesn't work hard.	B believes in him-/herself.	C will keep a secret.
7	A positive person	A sees the good in everything.	B is frightened of the future.	C is often bored.
8	A talented person	A has got a lot of money.	B isn't good at sports.	C is good at something.

2 ★★☆ **Read the text. Complete the adjectives. The first and last letters are given.**

My ideal friend is very ⁰a**ctiv**e – that's important because I play a lot of sports and I want him to play basketball in my team. He's ¹l_____-_____k and knows how to have fun, so he's a good person to hang out with. I need a friend who's really ²t_____d with computers, because I'm not good at IT and he could help me. Maybe it would be good if he was ³c_____g too – I'm not very ⁴c_____t, so he can help me talk to girls! (I know – I need to be more ⁵p_____e, right?)

3 ★★★ **Write one or two sentences about people you know (friends or family). Use adjectives from Exercises 1 and 2.**

_____
_____
_____
_____

Collocations `SB p.17`

4 ★☆☆ **Complete the text with the words in the list.**

~~won~~ | write | do | signed | missed | have

Last year, Jason's band were on TV – they ⁰ _____won_____ a talent show. Jason was a bit unhappy because his mum ¹_____ the show (she was ill). But the band members are very excited because they've just²_____ a contract with a record company.

The band members are talented musicians – they ³_____ all their own songs. They're hoping to ⁴_____ a lot of success on the music scene. Tomorrow morning, Jason is going to ⁵_____ an interview on TV.

5 ★★☆ **Complete the text. Use the correct forms of the verbs in A and the words in B.**

A ~~have~~ make (x2) sign do

B ~~a party~~ albums a degree a cake his autograph

The members of Jason's band ⁰ _are having a party_ to celebrate. Jason's mum has ¹_____. Some of the band's friends are asking Jason to ²_____ on their T-shirts. Cherie, the singer, is still planning to ³_____ in music at university next year, but says she can still ⁴_____ with the band.

WordWise `SB p.19`
Phrases with *just*

6 ★★☆ **Tick (✓) the five sentences that can be completed by adding *just*.**

0	I've … cleaned the floor.	✔
1	That horror film, *The Blob*, is … terrifying.	☐
2	He can't tell you if you don't … ask.	☐
3	This dress is almost … perfect.	☐
4	The flower show was … amazing.	☐
5	He's … a child, but he's a talented artist.	☐
6	No problem, it was … a thought.	☐
7	Gemma has … phoned. She's on her way.	☐

7 ★★☆ **Match the sentences in Exercise 6 with the meanings of *just*.**

1	a short time ago	0	☐
2	only	☐	☐
3	really	☐	☐

READING

1 REMEMBER AND CHECK **Match the people with the statements. Then check your answers in the online survey on page 13 of the Student's Book.**

1 Bia's mum

2 Mr Donaldson

3 Alex's grandmother, Gwen

4 Uncle Jack

☐	a	spends a lot of time away from home.
☐	b	has just done a parachute jump for charity.
☐	c	is very laid-back.
☐	d	devotes all his time to his family.
☐	e	is a wildlife photographer.
☐	f	is a seriously talented guitarist.
☐	g	has three children.
☐	h	has been on TV.
☐	i	is 78 years old.
☐	j	never complains.
☐	k	is a music teacher.
☐	l	thinks life is for living.

2 **Read the article. Tick (✓) four jobs that it mentions.**

1 comedian ☐

2 film star ☐

3 songwriter ☐

4 novelist ☐

5 singer ☐

6 translator ☐

3 **Read the article again. Mark the sentences T (true) or F (false).**

0 Joseph Conrad started to learn English when he was twenty. `F`

1 Conrad spoke English like an English person. ☐

2 Conrad's novels aren't very good. ☐

3 Victor Borge was a talented musician as a child. ☐

4 Borge learned English at school. ☐

5 Borge was a comedian on TV in the USA. ☐

6 ABBA were from Switzerland. ☐

4 **Do you know any other people who do things incredibly well in a language that isn't their first language? Who?**

AMAZING LEARNERS OF ENGLISH

We all know that a lot of people – and I mean a *lot* of people – learn another language and get really good at it. I'm not including bilingual people whose parents speak different languages to them from when they're born. (They're lucky – they don't even have to try, right?) No, I mean people who learn at school or even later and then get so good at their second language that they become famous in it.

Here's an example: a Polish man called Joseph Conrad. Well, his 'real' name was Józef Teodor Konrad Korzeniowski and he was born in 1857. When he was in his twenties, he became a sailor and started to learn English. Then he went to live in England. He stayed there for the rest of his life and he always spoke English with an accent. So what? Well, he changed his name to Joseph Conrad and he wrote novels in English. He wrote about twenty novels that a lot of people think are some of the greatest novels in English.

Another example? OK. Børge Rosenbaum was born in Denmark in 1909. He was an extremely good pianist – he gave his first concert when he was just eight years old! Later, he started to tell jokes when he played the piano and he became a piano-playing comedian – in Danish, of course. Then, when the Second World War started, he managed to escape from Denmark and he went to the USA. He was 31, he had $20 in his pocket and he spoke no English at all. So, to learn English, he watched films and went to watch American comedians. Then he changed his name to Victor Borge, started doing his own comedy acts and became a famous TV comedian – making jokes in his second language!

Then perhaps you can add the Swedish group ABBA, who became incredibly famous writing and singing songs in English. There must be others, but I don't know any more. Do you?

DEVELOPING WRITING

A person I know well

1 Read the text that Emily wrote about her friend Patrick. Match the pictures with three of the paragraphs.

A I'm going to write about one of my friends, Patrick. We met when he moved into a house in my street three years ago.

B He's a little older than me, but I always feel like he's much older! I think that's because he's a very confident person – he's only fourteen, but he's very sure of himself. When Patrick talks to adults, he talks to them like he's an adult too. He isn't afraid to disagree with adults, for example. I've never said 'No, I don't agree' to an adult, but Patrick has! I think that's a good point about him.

C Another good point is that he's very honest. If he doesn't like something, he says so. He never says 'Oh yes, it's great', just to be the same as everyone else. In fact, this is why some people at school don't like him very much, I think.

D Does he have bad points? Yes! He's forgetful. I remember a few times when he promised to do something, and he just forgot! Once he promised to come to my house and help me with something. He didn't come, so I phoned him. Like I said, he's honest, so he said, 'Oh, no. I forgot. I'll come right now.' And he did. He arrived with a big smile, saying, 'I'm awful, aren't I? I always forget. Sorry.' I couldn't be angry with him!

E I hope we're going to be friends for a long time.

2 How many good things and how many bad things does Emily write about?

_____

_____

3 Which adjectives describe Patrick? Tick (✓) three.

1	polite	☐	4	confident ☐
2	honest	☐	5	forgetful ☐
3	intelligent	☐	6	talented ☐

4 Look at the three boxes you ticked in Exercise 3. What examples does Emily give to show that these adjectives describe Patrick?

1 _____

2 _____

3 _____

5 Read the text again. Match the paragraphs A–E with the topics.

0	A not-so-good thing about Patrick	D
1	First good thing about Patrick	☐
2	Closing	☐
3	Who the person is	☐
4	Another good thing about Patrick	☐

6 Write about someone you know, perhaps a friend or a family member (150–200 words).

- Think about the person you're going to write about. How will you introduce them to your reader?
- What are the good things and what are the not-so-good things about them? In what order will you write about them?
- What adjectives are you going to use? What examples can you use to show what you mean by each adjective?
- How will you close your writing?

LISTENING

1 🔊 05 Listen to the conversation. ⟨Circle⟩ the correct words.

1 They're discussing *last weekend* / *going to a film* / *their parents*.
2 They both like *an actor* / *a film* / *London*.

2 🔊 05 Listen again. Mark the sentences T (true) or F (false).

0 Maggie thinks last weekend was exciting. ☐ T

1 A film premiere is the first time a new film is shown. ☐

2 Maggie wants to go the premiere of Liam Hemsworth's new film. ☐

3 Maggie thinks her parents will be happy for her to go. ☐

4 Jason has an aunt and uncle who live in London. ☐

5 Jason doesn't want to go to the film with Maggie. ☐

6 Jason doesn't like Liam Hemsworth. ☐

7 Jason and Maggie are going to talk to Maggie's parents. ☐

3 🔊 05 Listen again. Complete the conversations.

1 MAGGIE Well, you know that Liam Hemsworth is my absolute film hero?
  JASON Yes, ⁰ *of course I know* that. So ¹_____?

2 MAGGIE Well, I'm going to the premiere!
  JASON Oh, that's a ²_____!
  MAGGIE Oh? Do you really think so?
  JASON Yes, you ³_____ do it. You've always wanted to meet him.

3 MAGGIE Wow, that's great! Thank you. I'm just worried that my parents … ⁴_____, they won't like the idea.
  JASON I know what you mean. But, hey, you know what? You've got to ⁵_____!

Pronunciation

Sentence stress

Go to page 118. 🔊

DIALOGUE

1 Put the conversations in the correct order.

CONVERSATION 1

☐ A We can put a football match together between our street and Nelson Street.
☐1☐ A I've got an idea for the weekend.
☐ A Let's speak to some people about it now.
☐ B I'll come with you. We can do it together.
☐ B A football match? That's a great idea.
☐ B Yeah? What is it?

CONVERSATION 2

☐ A Thanks, but I'm not sure if we can do everything before Saturday.
☐1☐ A Julie, why don't we have a party?
☐ A I don't know. Can people come on Sunday?
☐ A Well, the next day's Monday – that's why. You know, homework to do, that sort of thing.
☐ B A party? Wow, yes! I'll help you if you want. Let's have it this weekend.
☐ B OK, so forget Saturday. But you should definitely do it. It could be Sunday.
☐ B Oh, don't worry about homework, Sue. Come on! You've got to make this happen!
☐ B Yes, I think they can. Why not?

PHRASES FOR FLUENCY SB p.19

1 Put the words in order to make expressions.

0 what / know *Know what?*

1 sure / you / are / ? _____

2 it / let's / face _____

3 that / and / that's _____

4 so / don't / think / I _____

5 of / sort / thing / that _____

2 Complete the conversations with the expressions in Exercise 1.

0 A Hurry up. The film starts at 8.30.
  B *Are you sure?* I heard it starts at 9.00.

1 A How did the tennis match go?
  B I lost. _____, I'm awful at tennis!

2 A So what did you do over the weekend?
  B Not much – read, watched TV, _____.

3 A Oh, Dad! Can I please watch *The Voice*?
  B No, you can't. I said no TV _____.

4 A I know it's raining, but let's go for a walk.
  B _____? I'm staying right here!

5 A This song's just fantastic.
  B Well, _____. It's terrible.

CAMBRIDGE ENGLISH: Preliminary

Writing part 1

1 For each question, complete the second sentence so that it means the same as the first. Use no more than three words.

0 Tennis is my hobby.

I really like *playing* tennis.

1 There are more than 100 people in my Facebook friends list.

I've _____ than 100 friends on Facebook.

2 Tom is a friend of my brother's.

Tom _____ friend.

3 I've just spoken to my mum on the phone.

I _____ my mum on the phone a few minutes ago.

4 Nigel's only two, but he can ride a bike.

Nigel has _____ to ride a bike and he's only two.

5 I'm always really interested when my granddad tells stories of the past.

My granddad's stories of the past are always _____ .

Exam guide: sentence transformations

In this section there are five questions about a certain topic. Each question contains a pair of sentences. The first sentence is complete. The second sentence says the same thing as the first sentence, but some words are missing. You have to write between one and three words to complete the gap in the second sentence.

- This question tests how well you know grammar. When you read through each pair of sentences, see if you can identify what the grammatical area is. This will help you focus on the answer. Common areas include *for* vs. *since*, comparatives and superlatives, *too* vs. *enough*, adverbs and adjectives and their opposites, *there is* vs. *have got*, etc.

- When you've written in your answer, read it 'out loud' in your head. Does it sound right? If not, rethink your answer.

- Does your answer mean exactly the same as the first sentence?

- Sometimes there may be more than one answer. Don't worry about this. Write in the answer you feel more confident about.

- Be careful with your spelling – you'll get no marks if you misspell a word.

- Make sure you write no more than three words or you'll get no points for the question, even if your answer completes the sentence correctly.

---

2 For each question, complete the second sentence so that it means the same as the first. Use no more than three words.

0 Tennis is my hobby.

I really like *playing* tennis.

1 This is my first time on a plane.

I've _____ on a plane before.

2 Buy your ticket today. It will be more expensive tomorrow.

If you _____ your ticket today, it will be more expensive tomorrow.

3 I've got a flight to Milan in the morning.

I'm _____ to Milan in the morning.

4 No car is more expensive than this one.

This is _____ car in the world.

5 You can buy your ticket on the train.

You _____ buy your ticket before you get on the train.

2 THE WAYS WE LEARN

GRAMMAR

Present perfect with *for* and *since* [SB p.22]

1 ★☆☆ Complete the sentences with *for* or *since* and a number where necessary.

0 Matthew has worked as a computer games tester ___*for*___ three years.

1 I've lived in this house _____ 2011.

2 We've had our pet rabbit _____ only six weeks.

3 Lauren has played the guitar in the band _____ she was 16 years old.

4 This tree has been here _____ more than 200 years!

5 I've written poems _____ I was ten years old.

6 Charlotte has been in the football team _____ 2013, so she has been a footballer _____ _____ years.

7 Joshua has played tennis _____ he was four years old. He was born in 2010, so he has played tennis _____ _____ years.

2 ★★☆ Write sentences. Use the positive and negative form of the present perfect and *for* or *since*.

0 Thomas / not see / grandfather / two months
Thomas hasn't seen his grandfather for two months.

1 Steve and Jane / be / singers / five years
_____

2 Sophie / not play / football / she broke her leg
_____

3 Harry / not write / on his blog / a long time
_____

4 Sam / not go / to the dentist / a year
_____

5 George and I / be / friends / we were kids
_____

6 They / not see / a good film / more than a month
_____

7 We / not go / on holiday / two years
_____

3 ★★☆ Jessie wants to ask her friends some questions for a school project. Complete them with the present perfect form of the verbs.

1 How long ___*have you lived*___ (live) in your house?

2 What is your best friend's name? How long _____ (know) him/her?

3 How long _____ (be) at this school?

4 What's your favourite possession? How long _____ (have) it?

4 ★★★ Look at the table and write answers to Jessie's questions. Use the present perfect and *for* or *since*.

	Emily	Jack	Dan
1	ten years	2010	three months
2	Sarah, 2009	Harry, 2012	Jim, a long time
3	five years	2012	September
4	bike, six months	dog, two years	laptop, May

1 Emily *has lived in her house for ten years.*

2 _____

3 _____

4 _____

1 Jack _____

2 _____

3 _____

4 _____

1 Dan _____

2 _____

3 _____

4 _____

5 ★★★ Answer the questions in Exercise 3 for you.

1 _____

2 _____

3 _____

4 _____

a, an, the or no article SB p.25

6 ★☆☆ (Circle) the correct words.

Yesterday I went to ⁰*the* / *an* park. I go there a lot, so I know ¹*a* / *the* park very well. I sat on ²*a* / *the* grass and started to read my book. Then lots of ³*the* / – things started to happen.

You can do lots of things in the park, but ⁴*the* / – bicycles aren't allowed. There was ⁵*a* / *the* boy on ⁶*a* / *the* bicycle who was riding on the path. ⁷– / *The* park keeper started to run after ⁸*a* / *the* boy on the bike, but she couldn't catch him.

There were three small boys playing ⁹– / *the* football in the park too, and when one of them kicked ¹⁰*a* / *the* ball, it hit ¹¹*a* / *the* boy on the bicycle and he fell off his bike. So the park keeper got him! I think this is ¹²*an* / *the* example of ¹³– / *the* really bad luck!

7 ★★☆ Complete the text with *a, an, the* or – (no article).

People have kept ⁰_____—_____ cats as pets for thousands of years. Cats are ¹_____ good example of how ²_____ animal can help ³_____ people, by catching ⁴_____ rats and ⁵_____ mice, for example. This is probably ⁶_____ most important reason ancient people had ⁷_____ cats. These days, many people have a cat at home, but they only keep it for ⁸_____ pleasure. Sometimes the cat sits on ⁹_____ owner's chair or knee, and the owner gets ¹⁰_____ pleasant feeling when that happens.

8 ★★☆ Read the sentences. Tick (✓) the four that are correct.

1 I love the dogs. ☐
2 I saw a beautiful dog in the park yesterday. ☐
3 The dog in the park was bigger than mine. ☐
4 It was standing beside the very small dog. ☐
5 I think the small dog was a Chihuahua. ☐
6 I think the dogs make really good friends. ☐
7 There are many different sizes of the dogs. ☐
8 I saw a picture of the biggest dog in the world. ☐

Pronunciation

Word stress

Go to page 118.

9 ★★★ Read Exercise 8 again. Change the four incorrect sentences so that they are correct.

1 _____
2 _____
3 _____
4 _____

GET IT RIGHT!

a(n) and no article

Learners often use *a(n)* where no article is needed, and no article where *a* is needed.

✓ I had **a** great time with my friends last Saturday.
✗ ~~I had great time with my friends last Saturday.~~

Complete the sentences with *a(n)* or – no article.

0 I've got *a* pet cat.
1 My brother works as _____ chef in a hotel.
2 Do you need to book _____ accommodation?
3 We haven't had _____ holiday for ages.
4 I am _____ student at the University of London.
5 We need _____ information about this urgently.
6 I would like to buy _____ desk and chair.

VOCABULARY

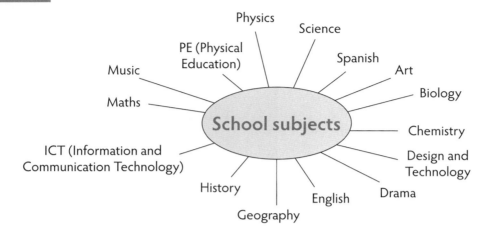

Physics
Science
PE (Physical Education)
Spanish
Music
Art
Maths
Biology
School subjects
Chemistry
ICT (Information and Communication Technology)
Design and Technology
History
Drama
Geography
English

Thinking

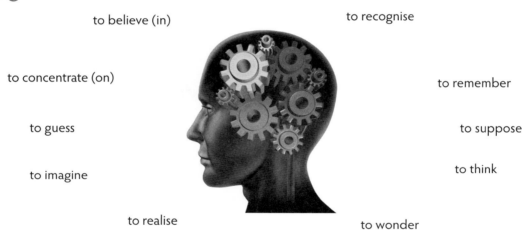

to believe (in)

to recognise

to concentrate (on)

to remember

to guess

to suppose

to imagine

to think

to realise

to wonder

Key words in context

achieve	I've worked hard all day, but I don't think I've really **achieved** anything!
away match	Our team is from London. Tomorrow they're playing an **away match** in Manchester.
encourage	His parents **encouraged** him to be a doctor, but he only wanted to be an actor.
exhausted	After working hard for twelve hours, she was **exhausted**.
motivation	He doesn't like his job. He hasn't got any **motivation** to work hard.
performance	It was his first time on the stage, and he gave a great **performance**.
planet	The nearest **planet** to Earth is Venus.
safety	**Safety** is very important in schools and that's why children aren't allowed to do anything dangerous.
strengthen	I did a lot of exercises to **strengthen** my arms.
teamwork	We all work very well together – it's great **teamwork**!
tool	Computers are an important **tool** for scientists.
warm-up	The players have a ten-minute **warm-up** before the game begins.
weight training	He does **weight training** and now he can lift 140 kilograms.
workshop	We went to a one-day **workshop** on 'How to look after your dog'.
youth club	The **youth club** in our town is a great place for teenagers to go to.

School subjects `SB p.22`

1 ★☆☆ **Put the letters in order to make school subjects.**

0   You probably need a piano if you're a (sciuM) teacher. _Music_

1   We often use computers in Design and (Thecloongy). _____

2   (regGyhoap) teachers don't need maps now that there's Google Earth. _____

3   We have our (stiChryme) lessons in one of the science labs. _____

4   Our Spanish teacher comes from Madrid. She never speaks (shEling) in class. _____

5   A calculator can be useful in a (thaMs) class. _____

6   I really enjoy (troyisH) lessons when they're about people, not just dates. _____

7   Our (amarD) teacher has been on TV and acted in a film! _____

2 ★★☆ **Look at the photos. Write the subjects.**

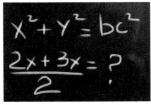

0   _Maths_   1   _____

2   _____   3   _____

4   _____   5   _____

6   _____   7   _____

Thinking `SB p.25`

3 ★☆☆ **Find the ten words about thinking.**

W	R	U	O	R	T	G	K	O	B	R
C	O	N	C	E	N	T	R	A	T	E
S	G	F	G	M	I	K	E	E	Y	B
G	T	E	U	E	E	B	A	S	E	T
I	H	G	E	M	I	H	L	I	H	I
M	I	N	S	B	E	L	I	E	V	E
A	N	S	S	E	L	V	S	Y	K	E
G	K	G	L	R	T	E	E	N	Q	L
I	F	V	U	J	X	O	L	O	K	E
N	S	U	P	P	O	S	E	G	F	L
E	U	O	M	B	W	O	N	D	E	R
P	R	E	C	O	G	N	I	S	E	C

4 ★★☆ **Complete the text with the words in Exercise 3.**

Do you ^{0}b_elieve_ _____ in the idea of morning people and night people? I do. I've always found it difficult to ^{1}c_____ in the morning. I can never ^{2}r_____ anything when we have a test in the morning.

I ^{3}w_____ why schools don't start in the evening. I ^{4}t_____ night people would love that. Can you ^{5}i_____ starting school at 8 pm? Great! We could sleep all day! But I ^{6}s_____ morning people would hate studying at night.

You can always ^{7}r_____ morning people – they're so cheerful in the mornings and don't seem to ^{8}r_____ that night people don't want to chat! So, am I a morning person or a night person? You can ^{9}g_____ , can't you?

5 ★★☆ **Read and answer the questions.**

1   Do you believe everything you read in magazines?
_____
_____

2   What kind of thing(s) do you remember easily?
_____
_____

3   What time of day do you concentrate best?
_____
_____

4   What do you imagine you will be in the future?
_____
_____

READING

1 REMEMBER AND CHECK (Circle) the correct words. Then check your answers in the article on page 21 of the Student's Book.

0 Tinkering School has a (summer)/ winter programme for kids.

1 At the school, kids learn life skills by *writing texts / building things* together.

2 Some children once built a bridge using *trees / shopping bags*.

3 Kids at the school don't suffer serious injuries because *there are health and safety regulations / they can't use knives or hammers.*

4 The 'real' school – Brightworks – has got *between six and 13 / only 20* students.

5 Most newspaper articles about Brightworks have been *critical / positive*.

6 Some people think the kids at Brightworks don't *learn / play* enough.

7 Since she started at the school, Tina Cooper *hasn't had to work hard / has never been bored.*

2 Read about Sunaina's first day at a new school in a new country. Answer the questions.

0 How did she feel about the school at the end of the first day?
She couldn't wait to leave.

1 What things made her feel bad?
_____

2 What surprised her most about the school?
_____

3 How does she feel about the school now?
_____

4 What has she learned from being at this school?
_____

3 Read the text again. Match these phrases with the correct places (A–H).

0	at the same time	*B*
1	but I sat by myself	☐
2	missing my mum and dad	☐
3	but that wasn't possible	☐
4	took a deep breath and	☐
5	to the class	☐
6	all kinds of	☐
7	get to know me	☐

Sunaina's family left India and moved to the USA when she was 13. She had to start a new school …

I remember it really well. My parents drove me to the school and said goodbye to me. I (A) walked into the school.

I didn't know what to feel. I was excited and scared and a bit nervous, all (B). There were lots of other kids around. They were already in groups of friends, but none of them said hello or anything. It was a strange feeling for me, like I didn't really belong there. I wanted to be somewhere else, (C).

The first thing I had to do was register, so I went to a room in the school that had a sign saying 'Administration'. Suddenly, I felt like I was some kind of criminal. They started asking me (D) questions. Then I went off to my first class.

My first class. Wow, that was horrible. Perhaps it was because my hair or clothes were different, but everyone just looked at me in such a strange way. And just like when I arrived, no one came to talk to me. Incredibly, that's never happened: no one has ever taken the time to (E) or like me. I have friends because I made the first move to meet people.

Maybe the worst class that day, though, was Science. The teacher wasn't too bad. She introduced me (F) and showed me where to sit. But the other students? Well, they looked at me like I was a guinea pig or something they were going to use for an experiment. I hated every minute.

Then there was a break and I went to sit somewhere alone, (G). But I thought they'd want me to keep trying, so I tried to be more positive in the next class. Not so good, though. Everyone talked to other students, (H). At the end of the day, I couldn't wait to get out of there.

But, as time passed, things have got better. Now I'm doing fine and I get OK grades. I've learned lots of things – but not what the teachers teach. I've learned that I'm strong and brave. I've learned that I will succeed even if some things aren't the way I want them to be.

4 Underline two or three things Sunaina says that you find interesting.

5 Write two questions that you'd like to ask Sunaina. Then write what you think she'd say in reply.

0 Q *What's your favourite subject at school?*
  A *Science. I like IT too.*

1 Q _____
  A _____

2 Q _____
  A _____

DEVELOPING WRITING

An informal email

1 **Read the email. Tick (✓) the things Jed talks about.**

1 How he feels about his routine ☐

2 The things he likes to watch on TV ☐

3 Homework that he doesn't like to do ☐

4 A party for his birthday ☐

2 **Read the phrases from the email. Match them with the words that have been left out.**

0 … good to get your last email. `b`

1 … everything going well? ☐

2 … any chance of you coming? ☐

3 … would be great to see you here. ☐

4 … hope you can come. ☐

a I

b It was

c It

d Is

e Is there

Hi Tania,

How's it going? Good to get your last email – it was fun to read. I liked hearing about your life, your routine and stuff, so I thought I could tell you about mine.

So, what can I tell you? Most weeks are the same as other weeks, really. I guess that's true about everyone, though. Monday to Friday, well, they're school days, so that's a kind of routine. You know, get up at 7.30, go to school at 8.45, come home at 4.00 and do homework, then have dinner and go to bed. Well, that's kind of true, but, you know, lots of things make every day different, so I don't mind the routine. It's OK. Every day there are different lessons at school and different things on TV in the evening. Even the homework is different sometimes!

Anyway, I wonder how you're getting on at your new school. Everything going well? I'm sure it is – you know how to make new friends and get on with things, right?

By the way, it's my 15th birthday next month (Saturday 12th) and we're having a party. Any chance of you coming? Would be great to see you here. Hope you can come. Let me know, OK?

So, what was I saying about routine and things? Yeah, right, homework – and I've got some to do, so I'm going to stop here. But I really, really want to hear from you again soon, OK?

Take care,

Jed

---

3 **Read the email again. Find these phrases.**

0 What Jed says instead of *How are you?*: *How's it going?*

1 Two ways that Jed starts to talk about a different topic: _____ and _____

2 Three ways he checks that Tania is following him: _____ , _____ and _____

3 How he ends his email: _____

4 **Write an email to an English-speaking friend (150–200 words). Your friend wants to know about your weekends and your routines.**

- Think about how to start and finish your email.
- Think about how you can make your email friendly and chatty – for example, asking questions to check your friend is following you and/or leaving words out to sound more informal.

Writing tip: writing an informal email

- People email each other to send news, ask questions, get simple information, or just to keep in touch. Very often, people write as if they were talking to the person they're writing to.
- People often speak in short sentences, and they write in short sentences too.
- Start your email with a general *How are you?* question. Do you know other ways of saying *How are you?*
- Tell the reader straight away what you're writing about and why.
- In speaking, people use phrases like *you know* and *right?* to 'get closer' to the listener. You can do this in an informal email too.
- Find a nice, friendly way to finish your email, for example, *Take care* or *All the best* or (if you know someone very well) *Love from . . .* .

LISTENING

1 ◀))09 Listen to the conversations. Match each one with a photo. There is one photo that you don't need.

A ☐

B ☐

C ☐

D ☐

2 ◀))09 Listen again and answer the questions.

CONVERSATION 1

0 Where does Jimmy want to go?
He wants to go to the toilet.

1 When does he have to come back?
_____
_____

CONVERSATION 2

2 What is the girl's project about?
_____
_____

3 Does the man let the girl take the photo?
_____
_____

CONVERSATION 3

4 Where is the boy's laptop?
_____
_____

5 When can he use Joanna's laptop?
_____
_____

DIALOGUE

1 Put the conversations in order.

1

1	GIRL	Excuse me. Is it OK if I try this shirt on?
☐	GIRL	Really? OK. Can I take a size 8 too?
☐	GIRL	OK, thanks.
☐	GIRL	I think so. This is size 6.
☐	WOMAN	Well, I think it might be too small for you.
☐	WOMAN	Of course you can. Here's a size 8. OK. Tell me when you're finished.
☐	WOMAN	Of course. Have you got the right size?

2

1	MARK	Jamie, can I ask you something?
☐	MARK	Great, thanks. Oh – another thing.
☐	MARK	Well, I forgot to charge my mobile phone. Can I take yours?
☐	MARK	I understand. Thanks anyway.
☐	MARK	Can I borrow your jeans tonight – you know, the white ones?
☐	JAMIE	Sure. What is it?
☐	JAMIE	Sorry, no way! My mobile phone goes with me everywhere.
☐	JAMIE	Yeah, go ahead. I'm not wearing them.
☐	JAMIE	Another thing? What is it?

▰▰ TRAIN TO THiNK ▰▰

Thinking about texts

1 Read the text about Sunaina on page 22 again. ⊙ircle the correct option: A, B, C or D.

1 Where *wouldn't* you find this text?

   A in a magazine   **C** in a newspaper

   B on a website   **D** in a homework book

2 What is the main purpose of the text?

   A to complain about bad schools

   B to describe a personal experience

   C to entertain the reader

   D to persuade readers not to change schools

3 What is the best title for the text?

   A What I learned in a school that I didn't like

   B My first day at school

   C Good and bad teachers

   D How to do well at a new school

Help with reading: identifying text purpose

1 **Read the texts. What is the purpose of each one?**

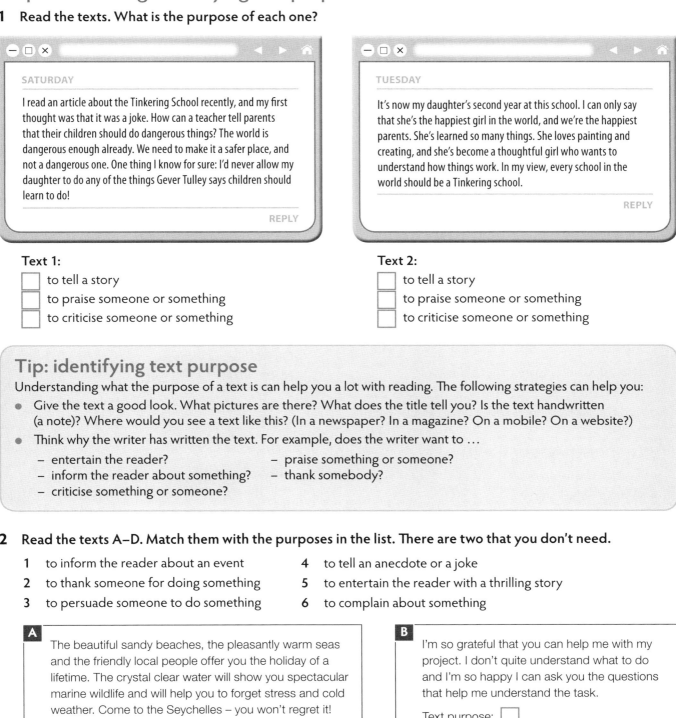

SATURDAY

I read an article about the Tinkering School recently, and my first thought was that it was a joke. How can a teacher tell parents that their children should do dangerous things? The world is dangerous enough already. We need to make it a safer place, and not a dangerous one. One thing I know for sure: I'd never allow my daughter to do any of the things Gever Tulley says children should learn to do!

REPLY

TUESDAY

It's now my daughter's second year at this school. I can only say that she's the happiest girl in the world, and we're the happiest parents. She's learned so many things. She loves painting and creating, and she's become a thoughtful girl who wants to understand how things work. In my view, every school in the world should be a Tinkering school.

REPLY

Text 1:
- ☐ to tell a story
- ☐ to praise someone or something
- ☐ to criticise someone or something

Text 2:
- ☐ to tell a story
- ☐ to praise someone or something
- ☐ to criticise someone or something

Tip: identifying text purpose

Understanding what the purpose of a text is can help you a lot with reading. The following strategies can help you:

- Give the text a good look. What pictures are there? What does the title tell you? Is the text handwritten (a note)? Where would you see a text like this? (In a newspaper? In a magazine? On a mobile? On a website?)
- Think why the writer has written the text. For example, does the writer want to …
  - entertain the reader?
  - inform the reader about something?
  - criticise something or someone?
  - praise something or someone?
  - thank somebody?

2 **Read the texts A–D. Match them with the purposes in the list. There are two that you don't need.**

1 to inform the reader about an event
2 to thank someone for doing something
3 to persuade someone to do something
4 to tell an anecdote or a joke
5 to entertain the reader with a thrilling story
6 to complain about something

A

The beautiful sandy beaches, the pleasantly warm seas and the friendly local people offer you the holiday of a lifetime. The crystal clear water will show you spectacular marine wildlife and will help you to forget stress and cold weather. Come to the Seychelles – you won't regret it!

Text purpose: ☐

B

I'm so grateful that you can help me with my project. I don't quite understand what to do and I'm so happy I can ask you the questions that help me understand the task.

Text purpose: ☐

C

The room was a mess. 'We've got to look at everything in here,' said the detective inspector. 'Every little bit! We know the robbers were here before they broke into the bank.' 'You won't find anything, Inspector,' a deep voice suddenly said.

Text purpose: ☐

D

Unfortunately, I have to say that we were not happy with the service we got at your hotel at all. Our room was far too small and too expensive, the meals were too small and often cold, and your waiters were very unfriendly.

Text purpose: ☐

CONSOLIDATION

LISTENING

1 🔊10 **Listen and tick (✓) A, B or C.**

1 When did Sophie start at the school?
   A Wednesday ☐
   B Friday ☐
   C Thursday ☐

2 What is Sophie's favourite subject?
   A Science ☐
   B Art ☐
   C Spanish ☐

3 Where does Allan offer to take Sophie?
   A the library ☐
   B the school café ☐
   C the school gym ☐

2 🔊10 **Listen again. Answer the questions.**

0 How many days has Sophie been at the school?
   4

1 How does it compare to her old school?

2 Who is her favourite teacher? What does he teach?

3 Why is Sophie good at Spanish?

4 Where is the library?

GRAMMAR

3 **Correct the sentences.**

0 I've been at Bishops High School since five years.
   I've been at Bishops High School for five years

1 It's a biggest school in our city.

2 I've yet taken some important exams.

3 But I haven't got the results already.

4 I've yet decided what I want to study at university.

5 I want to study the Spanish.

6 Bess is the my best friend at school.

VOCABULARY

4 **Match the sentence halves.**

0 He's so brave.   *d*
1 Your brother's so laid-back. ☐
2 Have you heard Jim play the trumpet? ☐
3 My granddad's so active. ☐
4 Liam's the most positive person I know. ☐
5 Mr Harrington's really cheerful. ☐

a He's so talented.
b He's always doing something.
c He can see the good in absolutely everything.
d He isn't scared of anything.
e He's always got a big smile on his face.
f Does he ever get angry?

5 **Write the subject these students are studying.**

0 Oh, no! I've got paint all over my shirt. Mum's going to kill me.
   Art

1 I love acting in front of the rest of my class. It's so much fun.

2 The capital of Italy is ... is ... Oh, what is it?

3 Twelve percent of 200 is 24, isn't it?

4 I like learning about the past, but why do we have to learn all those dates?

5 I don't believe it. I've forgotten my tennis shoes.

6 I love doing these experiments. It's so much fun.

7 We're practising a song for the end-of-year concert.

DIALOGUE

6 **Complete the conversation. Use the words in the list.**

~~'ve decided~~ | Let's face it | and that sort of thing. | Know what? | That's a great idea.
just | I'll help you if you want. | Are you sure? | Of course you can.

JOSH	I ⁰ *'ve decided* to start a homework club.
CHLOE	A what?
JOSH	A homework club. It's so we can get together, discuss lessons, help each other with our homework, ¹_____
CHLOE	²_____ Can I be in it?
JOSH	³_____ I want you to be in it!
CHLOE	⁴_____ I could text some people.
JOSH	OK. Who are you thinking of?
CHLOE	What about Dave?
JOSH	Dave? ⁵_____ He's way too smart. He doesn't need our help. ⁶_____ , he won't want to join.
CHLOE	Yes, but he doesn't have many friends. Maybe he'd like to join to make friends.
JOSH	⁷_____ You might ⁸_____ be right.
CHLOE	I might.
JOSH	In fact, it's perfect. We help him make friends and he helps us with our homework. Chloë, you're a genius!

READING

7 **Read the text. Mark the sentences T (True) or F (False).**

0 Mrs Millington started teaching when she was 40. **F**

1 Although she's a good teacher, she needs a bit more experience. ☐

2 Students are well behaved in her lessons. ☐

3 She really loves the subject she teaches. ☐

4 She was a TV news reporter before she became a teacher. ☐

5 She usually reported from countries with problems. ☐

6 She stopped working as a journalist when she started a family. ☐

7 Although she's a brilliant teacher, she's sometimes a bit unfriendly. ☐

My Geography teacher, Mrs Millington, is a really amazing person.

She's in her late forties, but she's only been a teacher for the last three years. You'd never know she hasn't got very much experience because she's excellent in the classroom. You'd think she's been a teacher all her professional life. Students love going to her classes. She never has any trouble from any of them because her lessons are so interesting that everyone just listens to everything she says. She's so enthusiastic about her subject and she really knows how to make her lessons interesting.

The other day we found out her secret, the reason why she's so good. Before she was a teacher she spent more thana 20 years as a war reporter for a newspaper. She spent most of her life reporting from countries all over the world, and she learned so much about these places and the people who live there. She brings all these experiences into the classroom and makes us feel that we've visited these places, too. She loved her job, but when she was 43 she had a child and decided that her job was too dangerous for a mother. She also wanted to be near her own mother, who wasn't very well. That's when she made the decision to be a teacher. I'm so happy she did. She's such a warm and positive person that when you're in her lessons you don't even feel you're at school.

WRITING

8 **Research a person who is famous for doing charity work. Write a paragraph (about 80–100 words) about him or her. Include the following information:**

- who the person is
- what charity work he/she does
- what makes him/her so special

3 | THAT'S ENTERTAINMENT

GRAMMAR

Comparative and superlative adjectives (review) `SB p.32`

1 ★☆☆ Complete the table.

Adjective	Comparative	Superlative
big	bigger	0 *the biggest*
1 _____	taller	2 _____
3 _____	4 _____	the prettiest
expensive	5 _____	6 _____
7 _____	more interesting	8 _____
9 _____	10 _____	the most difficult
good	11 _____	12 _____
13 _____	worse	14 _____

2 ★★★ Complete the text with the correct form of the adjectives.

I've just been to see *Gravity* and I can say that it's
0 *the most amazing* _____ (amazing) film I've seen this year.
It's brilliant. The special effects are incredible. They're
1 _____ (realistic) than any other
special effects I've seen. You feel like you're in space
with the actors. I really like space films. I thought *Apollo 13*
was really exciting, but *Gravity* is even
2 _____ (exciting). Sandra Bullock and
George Clooney are two of 3 _____
(professional) actors in Hollywood and they do some of
the 4 _____ (good) work of their careers
in this film. Of course, the fact that George Clooney is
5 _____ (handsome) man in the world
helps! The film is on at the Odeon until Friday. Tickets are
6 _____ (cheap) in the afternoon than in
the evening and the cinema is 7 _____
(empty) then too. But whatever you do, don't miss it!

Pronunciation

Words ending with schwa /ə/

Go to page 118. 🔊

(not) as … as comparatives `SB p.32`

3 ★☆☆ Look at the information about two cinemas. Mark 1–5 T (true) or F (false).

	The Roxy	The Gate
price	£10	£8
number of seats	230	170
friendly staff	★	★★★
age of building	1920	1970
distance from your house	1.2 km	0.7 km
overall experience	★★★	★★★

0   The Roxy is more expensive than the Gate. [T]

1   The Roxy is smaller than the Gate [ ]

2   The Gate isn't as friendly as the Roxy. [ ]

3   The Gate is older than the Roxy. [ ]

4   The Roxy isn't as close as the Gate. [ ]

5   The Roxy isn't as good as the Gate. [ ]

4 ★★☆ Complete the sentences about the cinemas using (*not*) *as … as* and the adjectives.

0   The Roxy isn't *as cheap as* _____ (cheap) the Gate.

1   The Roxy _____ (friendly) the Gate.

2   The Gate _____ (big) the Roxy.

3   The Roxy _____ (modern) the Gate.

4   The Gate _____ (far) the Roxy.

5   The Gate _____ (good) the Roxy.

5 ★★★ Complete the second sentence so that it means the same as the first. Use no more than three words.

0   There has never been a film as good as *Titanic*.
Titanic is the ___ *the best* ___ film ever.

1   The film is disappointing compared to the book.
The film isn't _____ the book.

2   *Avatar* is the most successful film of all time.
No film has been _____ *Avatar*.

3   *Despicable Me 2* is funnier than *Despicable Me 1*.
Despicable Me 1 _____ as *Despicable Me 2*.

4   *Spider-Man* and *Superman* are equally bad.
Spider-Man is _____ *Superman*.

Making a comparison stronger or weaker SB p.33

6 ★★ ☆ **Look at the pictures. Mark the sentences X (not true), ✓ (true) or ✓✓ (the best description).**

0

Tim *Owen*

A	Tim is taller than his brother.	✓
B	Tim is a lot taller than his brother.	✓✓
C	Tim isn't as tall as his brother.	✗

1
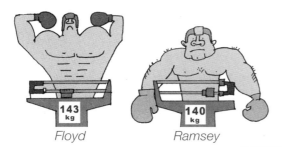
Floyd 143 kg *Ramsey* 140 kg

A Floyd is heavier than Ramsey.
B Floyd isn't as heavy as Ramsey.
C Floyd is a bit heavier than Ramsey.

2

£10 £100,000

A B isn't as expensive as A.
B B is much more expensive than A.
C A is cheaper than B.

3

Ellie TEST 99% *Ruby* TEST 13%

A Ruby's test was far worse than Ellie's.
B Ellie's test was better than Ruby's.
C Ellie's test wasn't as good as Ruby's.

7 ★★★ **Complete the sentences so that they are true for you. Use *a lot, much, far, a little* and *a bit*.**

0 I *am much shorter than* my best friend.
1 Maths _____ English.
2 Playing sports _____ watching TV.
3 Chocolate _____ apples.
4 Winter _____ summer.
5 Dogs _____ cats.

Adverbs and comparative adverbs SB p.34

8 ★ ☆ ☆ **Mark the <u>underlined</u> words ADJ (adjective) or ADV (adverb).**

0 He plays football <u>worse</u> than I do. *ADV*
1 Her German is <u>better</u> than mine. _____
2 He speaks <u>more clearly</u> than you. _____
3 You walk <u>more quickly</u> than me. _____
4 It's raining a lot <u>harder</u> today. _____

9 ★★ ☆ **Complete the sentences with the correct form of the words in brackets.**

'Why can't you be more like your cousin Kevin?' my mum always says.

0 He talks to adults *more politely* (polite) than you.
1 He studies _____ (hard) and always does _____ (good) than you at school.
2 His bedroom is _____ (tidy) than yours.
3 He eats _____ (quick) than you.
4 He writes _____ (careful) than you.
5 He treats me _____ (kind) than you.

GET IT RIGHT!
Comparatives and superlatives

Learners often incorrectly use *better* instead of *best* and *last* instead of *latest*.

✓ *Friday is the **best** day of the week.*
✗ *Friday is the ~~better~~ day of the week.*
✓ *I use the Internet to get the **latest** news.*
✗ *I use the Internet to get the ~~last~~ news.*

Ⓒircle the correct words.

0 This cinema always shows the *last / latest* films.
1 I don't think pizza is *best / better* than hamburgers.
2 Was it the *last / latest* one left in the shop?
3 It was one of the *best / better* days of my life!
4 He likes to wear the *last / latest* fashion.
5 It's the *best / better* restaurant I know.

VOCABULARY

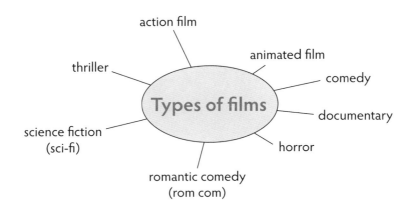

Types of films: action film, thriller, animated film, comedy, documentary, horror, science fiction (sci-fi), romantic comedy (rom com)

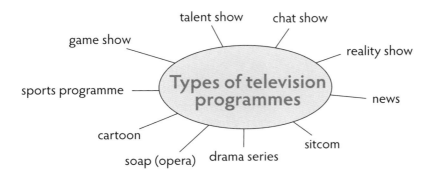

Types of television programmes: talent show, chat show, game show, reality show, sports programme, news, cartoon, soap (opera), drama series, sitcom

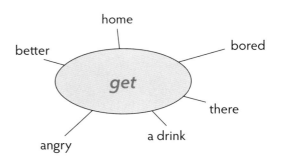

get: home, better, bored, there, a drink, angry

Key words in context

contestant	My mum was a **contestant** on a game show, but she didn't win anything.
crowd	There was a big **crowd** at the football game – more than 50,000 people.
enjoyable	I thought the film was really **enjoyable**. I liked it a lot.
equipment	You can make a film with very little **equipment** – a good video camera is all you need.
extra	They're making a film in my town and they're looking for 500 **extras**.
independent	She's very **independent**. She doesn't want help from anyone.
presenter	My brother is a children's TV **presenter**.
professional	George isn't very **professional**. He's often late for work and never replies to emails.
scary	The film was **scary**. I was really frightened.
scene	My favourite **scene** in the film is when the dragon attacks the castle.
script	The film has a great **script**. It's really well written.

Types of films SB p.32

1 ★★ **Read the clues and complete the crossword. Who is the mystery film character?**

This type of film …

0 is often set in the future or in space.

1 is always exciting, with lots of car chases, explosions and special effects.

2 makes you laugh.

3 is exciting and a bit scary at times too.

4 is always scary.

5 tells you about the real world.

6 is popular with children.

7 involves a love story and some laughs.

2 ★★ **Read the quotations. Write the type of film you think they come from.**

0 'Quick! We've got 60 seconds to stop the bomb from exploding!' *action film*

1 'Deep in the caves of Colombia lives a bird that few people have ever seen.' _____

2 'The next Mars shuttle leaves at 15.00. Meet me at the space station.' _____

3 'Come on, Barney Bear. We've got a problem to solve.' _____

4 'I love you, Thomas. I've always loved you. You're just too stupid to know that!' _____

5 'Did you see its face? I tell you – that thing isn't human!' _____

6 'It was a rainy Thursday evening in New York – the perfect time for a murder.' _____

7 'Why would I want to be a member of a club that would have me as a member?' _____

Types of television programmes SB p.35

3 ★★ **Put the letters in order to make types of TV programmes.**

0 thac hows *chat show*

1 swen _____

2 elyairt ohws _____

3 madra eiress _____

4 nocrato _____

5 mage wohs _____

6 cimtos _____

7 opsa proae _____

8 roptss magroprem _____

9 latent whos _____

The crossword:

```
      0 S C I F I
      1
      2
    3
          4
      5
      6
      7
```

4 Write the types of TV programmes.

WHAT'S ON?

0 'Tonight there's live action from Anfield, where Liverpool play Manchester City.' *sports programme*

1 'Who will win the final of *The It factor*: Janice and her amazing dog Timmy or the boy band Welcome?'_____

2 'On the sofa tonight, answering Paula Nightingale's questions, is actor Lewis James.'_____

3 'Tonight on *Win It Or Lose It*, three more couples compete to win £50,000.'_____

4 'Catch up on today's stories from the UK and around the world. Followed by the weather.'_____

5 'Minnie has a chance to make things right between Ian and James, but will she take it?'_____

WordWise SB p.37

Expressions with *get*

5 ★ **Complete the sentences.**

0 The show doesn't finish until 11 pm, so I don't think we'll get h*ome* before midnight.

1 I don't know how to get t_____, so I need to look at the map.

2 If you don't want him to get a_____, don't ask about the football match. They lost again.

3 You look really thirsty. I'll get you a d_____.

4 After a week in hospital, he got b_____.

5 It's an exciting film. You won't get b_____.

6 ★★ **What does *get* mean in each sentence?**

0 Call when you get there. *arrive*

1 Don't get too excited. _____

2 I need to get new jeans. _____

3 Where did you get that idea? _____

4 What did you get for your birthday? _____

READING

1 `REMEMBER AND CHECK` **Answer the questions. Then check your answers in the article on page 31 of the Student's Book.**

0 How much older is *Titanic* than *Spider-Man 3*? *Titanic is ten years older than Spider-Man 3.*

1 How much cheaper to make was *Titanic* than *Spider-Man 3*? _____

2 How many films did Moviefone consider better than *Monsters* in 2010? _____

3 What was the total cost of the cameras, film, etc. for *Monsters*? _____

4 How many people did it take to make *Monsters*? _____

5 How many main actors are there in the film? _____

6 How long did Edwards spend working on the film after filming? _____

7 How long is *Monsters*? _____

2 **Read the web page and comments. Which two films do the comments mainly talk about?**

THE MOST EXPENSIVE FILM OF ALL TIME (WELL, UP TO 2012)

1 *John Carter* (2012) – This Walt Disney epic cost around $300 million dollars. Unfortunately, neither critics nor audiences really liked it.

2 *Pirates of the Caribbean – At World's End* (2007) – This third film in the pirate story cost almost $300 million, but made more than three times that around the world.

3 *The Hobbit: An Unexpected Journey* (2012) – Each of the films in this Middle Earth fantasy trilogy cost about $250 million, meaning the total series cost near to $750 million.

4 *Tangled* (2010) – At $260 million, this Disney animation more than doubled its money, as audiences and critics loved it.

5 *Spider-Man 3* (2007) – It cost about $260 million. The critics hated it, but it still made nearly $900 million at the box office.

How can anyone justify spending so much money on a film? There are so many better things we could spend our money on: better roads, housing for everyone, looking after our environment, etc.
Jazzfan

👍 👎 LIKE · COMMENT · SHARE

Jazzfan – you're missing the point. Firstly, it isn't our money. It's the film studio's money, so they can spend it on what they want. Secondly, most of these films (except *John Carter* so far) have gone on to make loads of money for the studio. They're good economic investments.
Cottonbud

Why does it cost so much money to make an animated film? I mean, I really enjoyed *Tangled*, but I can't see how it cost $260 million!
Johnboy

Johnboy – Have you ever seen the credits at the end of an animated film? There are so many people involved. They all need to get paid. Also, they probably paid the storywriters a lot. It costs a lot to get a good story.
Cottonbud

I agree, Cottonbud. The writing in *Tangled* is brilliant. I took my kids to see it thinking it was just a film for children, but I was wrong. As a 35-year-old, I loved it. It made me laugh out loud several times. Much better than any of the other films on this list.
Johnboy

I can't believe they spent so much money on *John Carter*. What a waste of money – all special effects and no story. It was so bad that it made me laugh.
Liam86

Disagree with Liam86. Thought *John Carter* was fabulous – a good old-fashioned adventure film with brilliant special effects. Loved it! It reminded me of the films I watched as a boy. Don't understand why it didn't make any money.
OllieClarke

3 **Read the comments again. Mark the sentences T (true) or F (false).**

0 Jazzfan doesn't approve of lots of money being spent on a film. `T`

1 Cottonbud says film studios need to make money. ☐

2 Cottonbud lists three reasons why animated films cost a lot to make. ☐

3 Johnboy was surprised he liked *Tangled*. ☐

4 Johnboy found *Tangled* very funny. ☐

5 Liam86 describes *John Carter* as a comedy. ☐

6 OllieClarke says *John Carter* made him remember his childhood. ☐

4 **Choose one of the comments and write a reply (about 20–30 words).**

DEVELOPING WRITING

Discursive essay: for and against

1 Read the essay. Does the writer agree or disagree with the title? _____

'Watching television is a waste of time.' Discuss.

A Love it or hate it, television is a part of our lives. Parents use it as a babysitter for their children, teenagers watch it so they can discuss it with their friends at school and many old people depend on it for company. We all watch it, but are we really just wasting our time?

B TV is certainly an easy way of passing the time. All we have to do is turn it on and watch. It's easier than reading a book or doing exercise. It can make us lazy and it can become addictive. *Furthermore*, many programmes don't do anything to improve our lives. There are many arguments to support the idea that we waste too much time watching TV.

C *However*, in our busy lives we need time to relax and forget our problems. TV is the perfect way of doing this. *Moreover*, not all programmes on TV are rubbish. There are plenty of programmes that teach us things and make us think. If we choose the right programmes, TV can be a very good use of our time.

D *Personally*, I don't think we can say that watching TV is always a waste of time. Of course, it's very easy to waste a lot of time watching it, time that we could use for doing more useful things. *In my opinion*, if we plan what we watch and keep control over how much we watch, sensible TV viewing can be an important part of our lives.

2 Look at the words in *italics*. Which …

1 two expressions are used to say what you think?
Personally and _____

2 two words are used to add another argument?
_____ and _____

3 word is used to give an opposing argument? _____

3 Match the paragraphs with the purposes.

0 arguments to support the title `B`

1 arguments against the title ☐

2 the writer's own opinion ☐

3 an introduction to the topic ☐

4 Decide whether the arguments refer to statements A or B and whether they are for or against.

A 'Going to the cinema is always better than watching a DVD at home.'

B 'Film stars get paid too much money.'

	A or B	For	Against
0 They work really hard.	B		✓
1 We need to support our local cinemas.			
2 You can stop and start when you want.			
3 No one should get that amount of money.			
4 They make the film companies a lot of money.			
5 You can watch it as many times as you want.			
6 Films always look better on a big screen.			

5 Choose a statement from Exercise 4. Write an essay (about 200 words).

● Your introduction should make an impact. It shouldn't say what your opinion is.

● One paragraph should support the title and one should argue against it.

● Use the conclusion to give your opinion.

LISTENING

1 🔊13 Listen to the conversations. Match them with the pictures.

A 4

B [ ]

C [ ]

D [ ]

2 🔊13 Listen again and answer the questions.

0 Why does the man change his mind about getting some help?
Because he drops the TV and wants to help clear it up.

1 Why can't the man open the web page?

_____

2 What DVD does the shop assistant recommend?

_____

3 Why won't the TV work?

_____

DIALOGUE

1 Put the words in order to make requests and offers.

Offers

0 any / help / you / do / need
Do you need any help ?

1 help / I / you / can

_____ ?

2 OK / everything / is

_____ ?

Requests

3 something / you / help / could / with / me

_____ ?

4 hand / lend / you / me / can / a

_____ ?

5 few / you / minutes / got / have / a

_____ ?

2 Match the offers and requests in Exercise 3 with the replies.

a No, I'm all right. [ ]

b Sure – what is it? [ ]

c I do, actually. [0]

d Not really. I can't get the TV to work. [ ]

e Of course I can. [ ]

f Sure. Now, let me see. [ ]

3 Write a short conversation about the picture.

PHRASES FOR FLUENCY

1 Put the conversation in the correct order.

[ ] **ANNA** I always knew I would be. In fact, I had a dream about it when I was a little girl.

[ ] **ANNA** Well, this one did!

[1] **ANNA** Guess what? I've got a part in a soap opera!

[ ] **ANNA** I am. Have a look. It's a letter from the TV company.

[ ] **PAUL** What? You aren't serious!

[ ] **PAUL** Oh, come on! Dreams don't mean anything.

[ ] **PAUL** Wow! It's true! Looks like you're going to be famous after all.

2 Complete the conversations with the phrases in the list.

~~Guess what?~~ | have a look | after all
In fact | Looks like | come on

CONVERSATION 1

A ⁰*Guess what?* I won the singing competition.

B Oh, ¹_____! You aren't a good singer. ²_____, you're terrible!

A You're just jealous.

CONVERSATION 2

A So did you fail the test?

B No, I got 95 per cent!

A What?!

B Here – ³_____ if you don't believe me.

A It's true!

B ⁴_____ I'm not stupid ⁵_____!

Help with listening: getting ready to do a listening activity

1 🔊 14 **Listen to some people talking about their hobbies. Match each of the speakers with two activities. There are two activities you don't need to use.**

1 Joanne `b` ☐
2 Marek ☐ ☐
3 Alessandra ☐ ☐
4 Jorge ☐ ☐

a going to the theatre
b going swimming
c going to the cinema
d watching films on the computer
e going to the sports centre
f playing a musical instrument
g going shopping
h going cycling
i talking to his/her friends
j writing his/her blog

Exam guide: preparing to listen

When you do a listening activity in class, it's a good idea to do some reading and thinking before you listen, to get yourself ready. Here are some ideas.

- Read the task carefully. Are you sure you know what you have to do?
- Read the list of things carefully. Perhaps say the words to yourself in your head (or aloud if you aren't in class) and picture the things in your mind.
- It can be a good idea to underline the important words (for example, *go to the theatre*). Listen for these words when you listen to the recording.

- Sometimes the words in the task aren't exactly the same as the words you're going to hear. Is there another way you can say, for example, *go cycling* or *go to the cinema*? Try to think of words that are associated with the things written in the task.
- Listening can be challenging. A little work before you listen can help you a lot and make you more confident when you start listening.

Now try Exercise 2. It's a different kind of task – but can you use any of these tips to help you?

2 🔊 15 **You will hear a girl, Maia, talking about television. Decide if each sentence is correct or incorrect. If it's correct, circle the letter A for YES. If it isn't correct, circle the letter B for NO.**

		YES	NO
0	Maia watches a lot of television.	A	Ⓑ
1	Her favourite programme is called *The Street*.	A	B
2	The programme is on two days a week.	A	B
3	All the people in the programme live in the same street.	A	B
4	The person she likes most is called Ted.	A	B
5	The customers in the shop get angry with him because he makes mistakes.	A	B

4 SOCIAL NETWORKING

GRAMMAR

Indefinite pronouns (*everyone, no one, someone*, etc.) `SB p.40`

1 ★☆☆ (Circle) the correct words.

> **The new XR4 has landed!**
>
> ○ It's ⁰(everything)/ something you could want in a tablet and more.
>
> ○ It's so simple that ¹no one / anyone can use it, but if there's ²everything / anything you don't understand, our technical team are waiting to help.
>
> ○ Its amazing network coverage means you have Internet access ³everywhere / somewhere you go.
>
> ○ If there's ⁴something / nothing you need to remember or somewhere you need to be, the alarm system will make sure you don't forget.
>
> ○ If you order before Christmas, there's ⁵nothing / everything to pay until March.
>
> ○ The new XR4 – ⁶someone / no one should leave home without it.

2 ★★☆ Complete the sentences with the words in the list.

~~anyone~~ | everyone | nowhere | somewhere
anywhere | anything | no one | something

0 This party's boring. I don't know _____anyone_____ .

1 I'm sure I've seen that man _____ before, but I can't remember when.

2 Sally's really enjoying her new school. _____ has been so friendly to her.

3 There are no seat numbers in this cinema – you can sit _____ you like.

4 It wasn't me. I didn't do _____ , I promise!

5 Have you spoken to Ian? There's _____ he wants to tell you.

6 There are no trees here, so there's _____ to hide from the sun.

7 It's a secret. Tell _____ !

3 ★★★ Complete the second sentence so that it means the same as the first. Use no more than three words.

0 Liz is really popular. *Everyone* likes Liz.

1 I'm really bored. There's _____ do.

2 Are you hungry? Do you want _____ eat?

3 There's danger everywhere. _____ safe.

4 The cat has disappeared. I can't find _____ .

5 He's following me. He's _____ go.

all / some / none / any of them `SB p.41`

4 ★☆☆ Match the sentence halves.

0 We've got hundreds of DVDs, but [c]

1 I've got a lot of pens, but [ ]

2 There were ten teams in the competition, but [ ]

3 Twenty students took the final test and [ ]

4 The dogs have already eaten, so [ ]

a all of them passed.

b don't give any of them more food.

c I've already watched all of them.

d none of them played very well.

e I don't think any of them work.

5 ★★☆ Complete the sentences with *all, some, any* or *none*.

0 I have lots of friends, but _none_ of them remembered my birthday.

1 I like most of his films, but _____ of them are awful.

2 I can't say which game I like best. I love _____ of them.

3 I invited all my classmates to the party, but _____ of them came.

4 He's got 2,000 stamps. _____ of them are very rare.

5 Three buses came, but _____ of them were full.

> ## Pronunciation
>
> **The short /ʌ/ vowel sound**
>
> **Go to page 119.** 🔊

Giving advice: *should(n't)*, *had better*, *ought to* SB p.43

6 ★ ☆ ☆ **Match the sentences with the pictures.**

0   You should buy it. It looks good on you.   `C`

1   We ought to leave now. It's going to rain.   ☐

2   You'd better see a doctor about that.   ☐

3   There's a lot to do. We ought to start now.   ☐

4   You shouldn't touch those. They might be hot.   ☐

5   We'd better hide – quick!   ☐

7 ★★ ☆ **Write advice using the phrases in the list.**

~~change to a better provider~~ | open it | delete it
attach it as a file | activate flight mode on your tablet
choose a good password for it | upload it onto your blog
go online and find it cheaper

0   My phone never has a signal.
    You'd better change to a better provider.

1   I don't know who this email is from and it's got a
    strange-looking attachment.
    _____

2   This email's got lots of important information in it.
    _____

3   The new One Direction CD is £15 in the shops!
    _____

4   The plane's about to take off.
    _____

5   This photo's really embarrassing. I don't want
    anyone to see it.
    _____

6   I need to send this photo to Bob.
    _____

7   This web page contains loads of my personal
    details.
    _____

GET IT RIGHT!

all vs. *everyone*

Learners sometimes confuse *all* and *everyone*.

Everyone is a pronoun that refers to a group
of people.

✓ In the cinema we bought popcorn for **everyone**.
✗ In the cinema we bought popcorn for ~~all~~.

All is used to modify a noun or pronoun.

✓ My family have **all** got mobile phones.
✗ My family have ~~everyone~~ got mobile phones.

Complete the sentences with *everyone* or *all*.

0   I hope *everyone* likes the cake I've made.

1   My friends have _____ got jobs.

2   There should be enough lemonade for us _____
    to have some.

3   Has _____ finished their work?

4   Does _____ that you know have a computer?

5   I would like to introduce myself to _____
    members personally.

6   After that, _____ of us got a ball and tried to
    balance it on our heads.

VOCABULARY

Word list

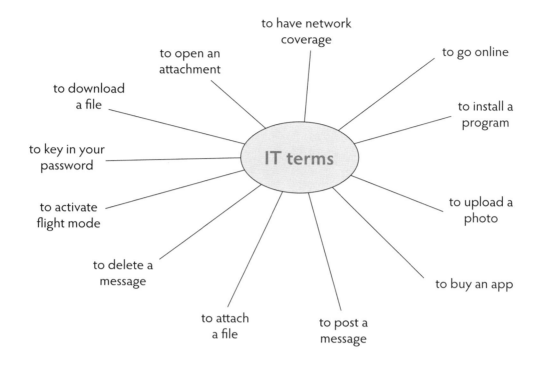

Language for giving advice

bad / good / practical / useful advice
advice on (something)
to ask for / get advice from (someone)
to give / offer (somebody) advice
to take / follow (someone's) advice
to ignore (someone's) advice
advisable
to advise (someone) (to do something)
to advise against (something)

Key words in context

account	I've got two email **accounts**. I use one for work and one for personal emails.
browse	Are you going to buy that book or are you just **browsing** through it?
cave	It was dark inside the **cave** and I couldn't see a thing. Luckily, I had a torch with me.
communication	There's no **communication** between them. They never tell each other anything.
emotion	My dad rarely laughs and I've never seen him cry. He doesn't show any **emotions**.
engrave	He has her name **engraved** on his ring.
get bullied	My sister **got bullied** at school, so she changed to another one.
invention	Is the Internet the greatest **invention** ever?
lick	He **licked** the stamp and put it on the envelope.
printing press	It's the oldest **printing press** in the country. It produced the first books in 1546.
publish	Our school newspaper is **published** every month.
social media	I think I'm the only person in the world who doesn't use any **social media** sites.

IT terms `SB p.40`

1 ★★ **Match the sentence halves.**

0 Before take-off, please activate — `d`

1 Don't open that — ☐

2 I haven't got any network — ☐

3 It's already Friday and I haven't posted — ☐

4 If you can't go to the shops, go — ☐

5 To open that file, you need to install — ☐

a a message on my blog yet.

b coverage, so I can't make a call.

c this program first.

d flight mode on your mobile devices.

e attachment. It could have a virus.

f online and buy it.

2 ★★ **Complete the sentence with an appropriate verb.**

8 steps to online security

1 Never _____ an attachment if you don't know where it's come from.

2 Think twice before you _____ a message on Facebook.

3 Don't _____ photos of people onto social media sites without asking them.

4 Be careful if you _____ in passwords in a public place.

5 Always _____ emails that you don't want other people to read.

6 Don't _____ apps from online stores you've never heard of.

7 Check what a program is before you _____ it onto your computer.

3 ★★★ **Complete the words.**

1 That's a great photo. You should u*pload* it to your s_____ m_____ pages.

2 If you like birdwatching, you should b_____ this a_____. It identifies birds from their song.

3 I forgot to a_____ the f_____ before I sent the email.

4 I've deleted the m_____ without reading it.

5 You need enter your email address and then k_____ in your p_____ .

6 It takes ages to d_____ big files.

Language for giving advice `SB p.43`

4 ★ **Write *advise* or *advice*.**

0 Don't take his *advice* . He doesn't know what he's talking about.

1 Our teachers always _____ us not to leave our homework until the last minute.

2 I must _____ you not to call her after 8 pm.

3 My mum always gives me good _____ .

5 ★ (Circle) **the correct option: A, B or C.**

The [0] *most* useful advice I ever got was from my grandfather. He said: 'Never take [1]_____ from anyone.' But I was only 18 and didn't know how good it was, so I [2]_____ his advice and let people give me advice [3]_____ everything. I [4]_____ advice on what to wear and what to eat. My bank manager advised [5]_____ save my money; friends advised me to spend it. My mother advised me to marry young; my father advised me [6]_____ it. I got so much advice [7]_____ so many people that I didn't know which advice to [8]_____ and which advice to ignore. My grandfather was right. Now I've stopped [9]_____ advice and life is much simpler!

	A	B	C
0	more	(B) most	much
1	advice	advise	advisable
2	took	followed	ignored
3	on	in	over
4	had got	got	had
5	to me	me to	me for
6	for	against	on
7	from	for	with
8	get	offer	follow
9	taking	giving	ignoring

6 ★★ **Answer the questions for you.**

1 What are you good at giving advice on?

_____

2 What's the worst advice you've ever got?

_____

3 Whose advice do you always follow and why?

_____

4 Are you good at taking advice? Why (not)?

_____

5 Do you like giving advice? Why (not)?

_____

7 ★★★ **Write about the best advice you ever got (about 50 words). Who gave it to you and why was it good advice?**

READING

1 REMEMBER AND CHECK Complete the sentences. Then check your answers in the article on page 39 of the Student's Book.

0 The man who lost his job because of social networking was ___20___ years old.

1 Around _____ people came to Cathy's party.

2 Every year, about _____ young people create problems for themselves because of social networking.

3 Rule _____ talks about keeping your online information safe.

4 Rule _____ suggests you should think before you post.

5 Rule _____ talks about the importance of good manners online.

2 Read the article. Write the names of the people under the pictures.

1 _____

2 _____

3 _____

3 Read the article again. Answer the questions.

> ## Be careful what you say

These days, with Internet sites like Twitter, it's very easy to let everyone know what you're thinking. But be careful what you say. It might get you into trouble, as it did for these three people.

In January 2010, Paul Chambers was lying in bed with a cold when he saw on TV that Doncaster Airport was closed because of snow. Paul had a flight from the airport the next week. Without really thinking, Paul sent a message on Twitter joking about blowing up the airport if it wasn't open soon. When he went to work on Monday, he found four police officers waiting for him at his office. He thought it was a joke, but when they took him to the police station and locked him up for eight hours, he knew it was serious. He went to court in May and had to pay nearly £1,000 for sending a threatening message.

Journalist Guy Adams was angry with the London Olympics on American TV. Because of the time difference between the US and the UK, the TV station NBC wasn't showing the sport live. Guy decided to tweet the email address of NBC's Head of Olympics, Gary Zenkel. He suggested that his followers tweeted and told Gary what they thought of his decision. When Guy tried to get into his Twitter account two days later, he found it was closed. He got an email a few days later telling him that he was no longer allowed to use the site.

!!!

Nicole Crowther was an actress in the popular US musical TV series *Glee*. She was an extra, which meant that although she was often in the show, she never said anything. However, on Twitter she regularly said things. In fact, she started giving away secrets about the programme. When the show's co-creator, Brad Falchuk, saw her tweets, he decided that she couldn't be in the show any longer. Nicole apologised and cancelled her Twitter account, but it was too late. She's now looking for other acting work.

?*@

0 Who tweeted another person's contact details? ___Guy___

1 Who lost a job because of Twitter? _____

2 Who did Twitter ban from using their site? _____

3 Who found themselves in trouble with police because of a tweet? _____

4 Who decided to stop using Twitter after the incident? _____

5 Who worried about the weather? _____

4 Complete the sentence with your ideas.

I think the story about _____ is the most interesting because _____

DEVELOPING WRITING

Computer advice

1 Read the blog entry and complete it with the words in the list.

~~tablet~~ | download | posted | blog | install | machine | deleted | online

Tipps for everyday life

Hi – I'm Johnny Tipp and welcome to my blog. Everyday life teaches me something. That's why I started this blog – so I could share it all with you.

Tipp 31 **What to do when your computer goes wrong**

I'm writing this post on my [0] _tablet_ because the desktop computer isn't working at the moment and everyone thinks it's my fault. But as I keep telling them, I was only trying to help.

Let me explain. A few days ago, I was writing my [1]_____ when a message appeared on the screen. It said there was a problem with the computer and that I should restart the [2]_____ . So I did. After five minutes, the same message appeared again. So I restarted it again. After about five times, I began to think this problem was serious, so I went [3]_____ to find a solution. I found a site that promised to fix everything.

TIP 1 **You should never trust anyone who promises to fix everything.**
All I had to do was [4]_____ a file onto my computer and then [5]_____ it. So I did.

TIP 2 **You should never download files from people who promise to fix everything.**
The next thing I saw was a message [6]_____ on the screen: 'To fix this problem, please enter your credit card details.' Well, for some reason, I know my dad's credit card details and so I entered them.

TIP 3 **Never pay anyone who promises to do everything before they do it.**
Then the computer just [7]_____ all the files on it and turned itself off and has never come on again since. So when Dad came home, all tired from work, I told him the whole story.

TIP 4 **Never tell bad news to a tired person.**
When he finally calmed down, he rang his bank. They found that £1,000 was missing from his account.

And that's it. It was an expensive lesson, but I've learned a lot.

PS I'm not the most popular person in my house at the moment.

2 Read the blog entry again. Put the events in order.

- [ ] Johnny tells his dad about the problem.
- [ ] Johnny writes his blog.
- [ ] Johnny installs a program.
- [1] Johnny's computer tells him it has a problem.
- [ ] Johnny's computer completely breaks down.
- [ ] Johnny goes online to try and find a solution.
- [ ] Johnny uses his dad's credit card.
- [ ] Johnny downloads a program.

3 Write a blog entry giving advice to your readers (about 200–300 words). Tick (✓) the checklist.

- [ ] 200–300 words
- [ ] chatty, informal language
- [ ] contains advice
- [ ] interesting content
- [ ] nothing too personal

Writing tip: writing a blog

- A blog is something that someone writes because they want to share some information with the rest of the world. Some blogs are about specific topics such as cycling or online gaming. Others are just about the everyday life of the author.

- Decide what your blog will be about. Do you have a special interest in something that you would like to share or do you just want to talk about your life?

- Your blog should be interesting. If it isn't, it won't attract many readers.

- If your blog is about your life, be careful not to give away personal information such as your address or phone number.

- Keep your blog chatty and informal. Write in a style that is appropriate to your readers.

- If you want to keep your readers, don't forget to update your blog regularly.

LISTENING

1 ◀))17 **Listen to the conversations. Match them with the computer screens.**

A □ B □ C □

Error 323

2 ◀))17 **Listen again and complete the notes.**

CONVERSATION 1
Problem: *The program keeps freezing.*
Solution: _____

CONVERSATION 2
Problem: _____
Solution: _____

CONVERSATION 3
Problem: _____
Solution: _____

3 ◀))17 **Listen again and answer the questions.**
CONVERSATION 1

1 What kind of computer does the man have?
_____

CONVERSATION 2

2 What kind of computer does the man have?
_____

3 When did the man buy it?
_____

CONVERSATION 3

4 What is the man's password?
_____

5 What does the man see on his screen?
_____

DIALOGUE

1 **Put the words in order to make sentences.**

0 we'll / better / do / shop / and / bring / the / machine / can / You'd / into / the / see / we / what
   You'd better bring the machine into the shop and we'll see what we can do.

1 read / use / You / to / you / computer / the / ought / before / instructions / really / the
   _____

2 anyone / tell / should / never / password / You / your
   _____

3 put / immediately / your / down / You / the / should / phone / call / bank / and
   _____

TRAIN TO THiNK

Logical sequencing

1 **Put the actions into a logical order.**

1
□ Ask for some advice
□ Get some bad advice
□ Take the advice
1 Have a problem
□ Get some good advice
□ Ignore the advice
□ Ask someone else

2
□ Send your message
□ Write a reply
□ Add an attachment
□ Delete the first message
□ Log into your email
□ Key in your password
1 Go online
□ Read a message

2 **Connect the first and last events in the lists with your own ideas.**

1
1 Find an old friend on a social networking site.
2 *Send the friend a message asking about their life.*
3 _____
4 _____
5 Delete the friend!

2
1 See a great new band on TV.
2 _____
3 _____
4 _____
5 Go and see their show.

Reading part 2

Exam guide: matching people with activities and things

- In this question you have to read short descriptions of five people and match them with the best options. The options relate to a particular subject, for example, the best holiday location, the film they'll like the most or the museum they'll find the most interesting.
- Read through the short descriptions of each person. Underline the important information in each one.
- Before you read through the options, think about what sort of thing you would recommend for each person.
- Read through the options and underline the most important information in each one. See if any match your own ideas.
- Beware of 'word spotting'. Just because the same word might appear in the description and one of the options, it doesn't always mean that this is a match. For example, just because Tom is going to India, it doesn't mean that theheartofindia.com is necessarily the best place for him.
- Always double-check and look carefully at all the information. Look out for traps. For example, Andy is looking for a recipe for hot and spicy food and goodenoughtoeat.com offers this, so you might think this is the perfect match. But look again. Andy wants to make a beef dish and this website is for vegetarians!
- Remember: there are always three extra options. These extra options will usually contain traps.

1 Match the people 1–5 with five of the websites A–H.

1 Liam is doing a school Geography project. He has to find out all he can about Russia, China, Brazil and India, and use the information to compare these countries. ☐

2 Tom is going on a two-month trip around India. He knows exactly what he wants to see and do, but he needs to organise how he's going to get around and where he's going to stay. ☐

3 Andy is cooking dinner for some friends tonight. He wants to make a spicy beef dish and needs a good recipe. ☐

4 Olivia has got to look after her two young children during the school holidays. She wants to find things to do in the local area that will get them out of the house. ☐

5 Miriam is taking her niece for a day out to the science museum in Manchester. She wants to drive there, but has no idea how to get there. ☐

HOT SITES – A pick of the best new websites this week

A fromAtoBandback.com
Everything from road directions to bus and train timetables. Just type in where you are and where you want to go and we'll tell you the best way of getting there. We also work out how long it'll take you to get there and how much it'll cost. You'll never need to feel lost again.

B goodenoughtoeat.com
Transform your carrots, cabbages, onions and mushrooms into wonderful meals that all the family will love. From soups to keep you warm in the winter to hot, spicy curries to impress your friends at any time of the year. We have a vegetarian recipe for every occasion. Say goodbye to meat!

C theheartofindia.com
India is one of the world's oldest and most magical civilisations. Our site is dedicated to 1,000 years of tradition. Everything you'll ever need to know about India is here: our history, our customs, our stories, our cities, our wildlife and our people. You'll also find the best recipes for curries anywhere on the web!

D wotson.com
Looking for a good film to see or show to go to? Want to know what exhibitions are on at the museums and art galleries in your area? Are there any special events taking place near you this weekend? Check out what's happening around you this month here.

E rentacar.com
If you're just looking for a small car for the day or a more luxurious model for the month, you won't find a better deal than here. Our cars all come freshly cleaned, full of petrol and with a satnav, so you'll always know where you are. For the best prices in town – we can't be beaten.

f thejourneyplanner.com
No matter where in the world you're going, we have all the information you'll need to plan the perfect holiday. Our site also searches the Internet to give you the best prices on accommodation, transport and eating out. Our simple booking form makes it easy for you to make all your reservations and take all the worry out of arriving.

g rainyday.com
Kids home for the summer? Rain pouring down outside? Don't worry. We have hundreds of ideas to keep your children active over the holidays. Perfect for those days when getting out of the house seems impossible. Turn off the TV and get busy.

h welcometotheworld.com
The Internet database for all 196 countries in the world. Facts and figures on everything from population size to life expectancy, from import and export to GDP. Find out how your country compares to the rest of the world.

CONSOLIDATION

LISTENING

1 🔊 **18** **Listen to the conversation. Tick (✓) A, B or C.**

1 What kind of show is *Priceless*?
  A a chat show ☐
  B a sports show ☐
  C a game show ☐
2 What kind of film is *Let Him Go*?
  A a sci-fi film ☐
  B a horror film ☐
  C a comedy film ☐
3 What time does the *Let Him Go* start?
  A 8 pm ☐
  B 9 pm ☐
  C 11 pm ☐

2 🔊 **18** **Listen again. Answer the questions.**

0 Why does Jim want to stay in?
  Because he's a bit tired.
1 What day of the week is it?
  _____
2 What kind of film is *By Tomorrow*?
  _____
3 What happens in *Let Him Go*?
  _____
4 What does Sally want Jim to make?
  _____

VOCABULARY

3 **Look at the word snake. Find 12 types of films and TV programmes and write them in the correct column. Some can go in both.**

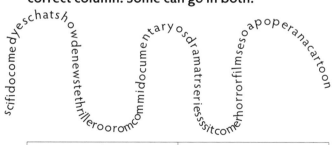

TV shows	Types of films
	sci-fi

4 **Complete the text with the words in the list. There are three words you don't need.**

~~buy~~ | download | attach | useful | on | post
against | open | ignored | for | followed | key

One of the problems with modern technology is the number of passwords you need to remember. Every time I want to ⁰ *buy* an app, check my email or ¹_____ a message on Facebook, I have to ²_____ in a password. My computer even sometimes asks for one if I want to ³_____ a file or ⁴_____ an attachment. What makes it worse is that all these passwords have to be different. So I asked a friend of mine ⁵_____ some advice. He advised me ⁶_____ keeping them on my computer. He told me to write them all down in a file and send it to myself and keep it in my email inbox. It sounded like ⁷_____ advice so I ⁸_____ it and did exactly what he said. So my passwords are all safely stored in my email inbox. The only problem is that I can't remember the password to access it!

GRAMMAR

5 **Rewrite the sentences using the words in brackets.**

0 I don't know anyone kinder than her. (kindest)
  She's the kindest person I know.
1 The film was hated by everyone. (no one)
  _____
2 You should study more if you've got a test tomorrow. (better)
  _____
3 The weather was a lot nicer yesterday. (worse)
  _____
4 Polly is nearly as tall as Angus. (a bit)
  _____
5 The best thing for you to do is to tell the truth. (ought)
  _____
6 Is this house empty? (anyone)
  _____
7 I'm a bad singer, but I'm better than Josh. (badly)
  _____
8 It's really important for me to finish this today. (must)
  _____
9 It's a good idea for us to leave early. (need)
  _____

DIALOGUE

6 **Complete the conversation. Use the phrases in the list.**

~~have you got a few minutes?~~ | looks like
Is everything OK? | Can you lend me a hand?
ought to | after all | I can do it for you
have a look | In fact

EMMA   Simon, ⁰ *have you got a few minutes?*

SIMON   Sure. Yes, I have. ¹_____

EMMA   Not really. I'm trying to download this file, but it isn't working. ²_____

SIMON   Of course. Let me take a look.

[after a few minutes]

SIMON   That's very strange. It ³_____ you've got a virus on your computer.

EMMA   A virus!

SIMON   Yes, ⁴_____ . Each time I try and open this window, it just shuts down.

EMMA   Oh no. Is it serious?

SIMON   Not really. ⁵_____ , I had the same one on my computer. I know exactly what to do.

EMMA   Great. So can you fix it?

SIMON   Yes, I can. I'm just running a program now. But you really ⁶_____ update your virus protection. ⁷_____ if you want.

EMMA   Thanks. That would be great.

SIMON   Oh. Oh dear.

EMMA   What?

SIMON   Well, it didn't do that before. It seems your computer's gone completely dead. Very strange. Maybe I didn't know that virus ⁸_____ .

READING

7 **Read the article and match the missing sentences with the spaces A–F. There is one sentence that you don't need.**

0	they watched the night before	B
1	in the house	☐
2	apart from things like live football matches,	☐
3	like they did when my parents were children	☐
4	whenever and wherever they like	☐
5	better sound and	☐
6	you didn't have a chance of seeing it again	☐

The end of television?

Does anybody sit down and watch TV these days? When my parents were growing up, they only had a few channels to choose from. If you missed your favourite programme, it was just bad luck – **[A]** (unless you had a video recorder and remembered to programme it). The TV was the centre point of the house. Families planned what show they wanted to see and cooked their dinners so that they could finish eating in time to watch it. At school, children talked about the shows **[B]** and because there weren't many programmes for kids, they all watched the same thing.

When I grew up, the TV was bigger and a lot thinner than the TVs of my parents' time. It had **[C]** a remote control to change between the many channels. But the TV was still an important piece of furniture **[D]** and we all sat around it on a Saturday night to watch something as a family.

These days, TV just doesn't seem to be so important, and **[E]** people can choose what they want to watch and when they want to watch it. They don't even need to watch it on a TV. They can download programmes and watch them on their tablets and phones **[F]**. Watching TV has become a much more individual activity and in many houses the TV set sits forgotten in the corner of the living room, waiting for the day when the family sits down together again and turns it on.

WRITING

8 **Write a short text (about 120–150 words) about your favourite TV programme. Include the following information:**

- what it is
- when it's on
- what it's about
- why you like it

5 MY LIFE IN MUSIC

GRAMMAR

Present perfect continuous `SB p.50`

1 ★☆☆ **Match the sentences with the pictures.**

0 He's been talking to them for hours. `B`

1 He's been waiting for a long time. ☐

2 It's been snowing for days. ☐

3 She's been running for 62 hours. She's trying to break the world record. ☐

4 They've been watching TV all evening. ☐

5 She's been playing her favourite instrument all morning. ☐

2 ★★☆ **Complete the sentences. Use the present perfect continuous (positive or negative) form of the verbs.**

0 She'*s been reading* (read) that book for more than a week now.

1 Dave's in bed. He _____ (feel) well for about three hours.

2 Dinner's going to be good. Dad _____ (cook) all afternoon.

3 What awful weather. It _____ (rain) all day.

4 She looks really tired. She _____ (sleep) very well.

5 I _____ (study), so I don't think I'm going to pass this test.

3 ★★☆ **Complete the text. Use the present perfect continuous form of the verbs in the list.**

~~try~~ | think | write | talk | dream

I ⁰ *'ve been trying* to contact you. Is your phone broken? I want to ask you a question: will you join 'The Cool Four'? Jason, Nora, Zoë and I have started a band! As you know, I ¹_____ songs for years, and I ²_____ of having my own band. I'm sure people ³_____ that I'd never do it. Well, they're wrong! Jason, Nora and Zoë are here now, and we ⁴_____ about the name of the band if you join us! How does 'The Cool Five' sound?

4 ★★☆ **Write present perfect continuous questions.**

0 `e` why / she / cry
   Why has she been crying _____ ?

1 ☐ how long / she / speak / to the teacher
   _____ ?

2 ☐ how long / you / try to phone me
   _____ ?

3 ☐ what / you / do
   _____ ?

4 ☐ how long / Bob / practise / the piano
   _____ ?

5 ★★★ **Complete the sentences. Use the present perfect continuous form of the verbs.**

a He'*s been playing* (play) since 10.30.

b I _____ (try) to reach you for two days.

c They _____ (discuss) the exam for an hour.

d I _____ (tidy) my room.

e She _____ (feel) sad about her cat.

6 ★★★ **Match the questions in Exercise 4 with the answers in Exercise 5. Write a–d in the boxes.**

Pronunciation

Strong and weak forms /biːn/ and /bɪn/

Go to page 119.

Present perfect simple vs. present perfect continuous `SB p.53`

7 ★☆☆ **Match 1–5 with a–f.**

0 He's been wearing these jeans for years. [f]

1 He's bought a new pair of jeans. ☐

2 She's been recording since 7 am. ☐

3 She's recorded all the songs for her new CD. ☐

4 They've been playing all evening. ☐

5 They've played concerts in many countries. ☐

a She's tired and hungry.

b They've got fans all over the world.

c But they're too big for him.

d But they haven't played their best song yet.

e She can go home now.

f He needs to buy a new pair.

8 ★★☆ **Complete the sentences. Use the present perfect simple or present perfect continuous.**

0 We*'ve been practising* all afternoon.
   We *'ve practised*_____ 20 songs. (practise)

1 We _____ at photos for hours.
   We _____ at all my albums! (look)

2 She _____ 50 messages today! She
   _____ emails since 8 o'clock. (write)

3 We _____ to songs all evening.
   We _____ to five albums. (listen)

4 They _____ the guitar since 1985.
   They _____ a lot of concerts. (play)

5 She _____ 300 pictures. She
   _____ for many years. (paint)

9 ★★★ **Write questions with *How long* and the present perfect simple or continuous.**

0 you / play / the piano
   How long have you been playing the piano ?

1 he / know / Ben
   _____ ?

2 they / play / in a band
   _____ ?

3 you / have / your guitar
   _____ ?

4 she / listen / to music
   _____ ?

5 they / be / teachers
   _____ ?

6 we / live / in this house
   _____ ?

10 ★★★ **Complete the questions. Use the correct form of the verbs in the list.**

~~know~~ | hear | be | play | study

0 How long *have you known* your best friend?

1 What's your favourite sport and how long
   _____ it?

2 What class are you in now and how long
   _____ in it?

3 How long _____ English?

4 What is the most interesting information you
   _____ today?

11 ★★★ **Write your answers to the questions.**

0 _____
   _____

1 _____
   _____

2 _____
   _____

3 _____
   _____

4 _____
   _____

GET IT RIGHT! ◉
Present perfect continuous vs. past continuous

Learners sometimes use the past continuous when the present perfect continuous is required.

✓ *I've been looking* for a new phone since last week.

✗ *I was looking* for a new phone since last week.

Complete the sentences with the correct form of the verb in brackets.

0 Over the last few weeks I*'ve been training* (train) for the race.

1 I _____ (eat) breakfast when I heard the news.

2 I _____ (wait) to see the latest *Star Wars* film for months.

3 She _____ (work) there last year, but she left in December.

4 I _____ (play) the violin for two years.

5 We _____ (get) this discount for the last three years.

6 I had to leave the meeting because my mobile phone _____ (ring).

VOCABULARY

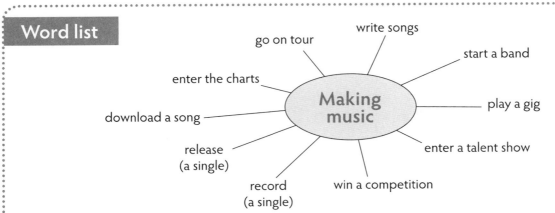

Making
music

write songs
go on tour
start a band
enter the charts
play a gig
download a song
release
(a single)
enter a talent show
record
(a single)
win a competition

Musical instruments

drums

bass guitar

saxophone

piano

violin

trumpet

keyboards

guitar

out

My dad **started out** making tea for the bosses. Now he's the boss of the company.

I only **found out** about his accident when I read about it in the paper.

The printer's **run out** of ink. We need to buy some more.

The new Minecraft game **comes out** next Friday. I can't wait.

Do you want to **go out** tonight? The cinema or a restaurant, maybe?

If you tell me what the problem is, we can **sort it out** together.

Key words in context

busking	In summer you'll hear a lot of **busking** in the streets of London.
concentrate	Music helps me to **concentrate** better on my work.
dance music	I like the rhythm of this song. I think it's good **dance music**.
entertaining	His performances are always very **entertaining**.
jazz	It was black people in the US who invented **jazz**.
lyrics	I don't understand the **lyrics** of this song. What do you think they mean?
melody	I like the **melody** of this song. It's really easy to sing along to.
musician	He's an excellent **musician**. He plays six instruments.
opera	Janet loves classical music, but she doesn't often listen to **opera**.
performance	It was a great **performance** by the band.
pop	What's your favourite **pop** song?
rap	In **rap**, they don't sing the words – they speak them.
rock	I prefer **rock** to pop.

Making music SB p.50

1 ★☆☆ **Complete the text with the words in the list.**

started a band | wrote / songs | recorded / single
download | played gigs | entered the charts
released | went on / tour

When Mick Jagger [0] *started a band* called The
Rolling Stones in 1962 with a few friends, he had no
idea how successful they would become. The Stones
[1]_____ their first _____, *Come On*,
a song by the singer Chuck Berry, and [2]_____
it on 7 June, 1963. They never performed it when they
[3]_____ because it wasn't 'their' song. But their
fans found out about the record, and so many people
bought it that it [4]_____ in the UK and went to
number 21. Of course, in those days, fans had to go to
record shops; they couldn't just [5]_____ music
from the Internet! Mick Jagger and Keith Richards
[6]_____ a lot of _____ that became very
famous. In 1964, The Rolling Stones [7]_____
their first _____ of the US. When they came
back, they had their first number one hit in the UK,
It's All Over Now.

Musical instruments SB p.53

2 ★☆☆ **Put the letters in order to make musical instruments.**

1 The _drums_ (sdmur) and the _____ (sabs
aitugr) are responsible for the rhythm in a band.

2 The _____ (rmutpte) and the _____
(nxohpasoe) are wind instruments.

3 _____ (ysedbaokrs) are electronic instruments
similar to a _____ (iaopn).

4 The _____ (linvoi) and the _____ (griuat)
are both examples of string instruments.

3 ★★☆ **Tick (✓) the sentences that are true for you. Correct the ones that aren't.**

1 I never listen to jazz. ☐

2 I prefer pop to rock. ☐

3 I like songs with good melodies. ☐

4 I don't really like rap. ☐

5 I never listen to the lyrics of a song. ☐

WordWise SB p.55
Phrasal verbs with *out*

4 ★☆☆ **Circle the correct option: A, B or C.**

0 We need help. Who could _____ this out for us?
   A come B start **C** sort D go

1 I'm afraid I'm _____ out of ideas. I'm not sure what to do.
   A coming B running C sorting D finding

2 I love _____ out with my friends.
   A finding B starting C sorting D going

3 My cousin _____ out writing for the local newspaper. Now he's a journalist on TV.
   A started B found C sorted D went

4 Nobody saw what happened, so it's difficult for the police to _____ out the truth.
   A come B run C go D find

5 They haven't had a new song for two years, but their new CD should _____ out soon.
   A sort B find C go D come

5 ★★☆ **Match the questions and answers.**

0 Why won't you join us at the cinema tonight? c

1 What if your dad finds out about it? ☐

2 When did this book come out? ☐

3 What was your brother's first job? ☐

4 Can I talk to Jane? ☐

5 We have a real problem with this. ☐

a I can't remember. I bought it a long time ago.

b Oh, don't worry. I'm sure we'll sort it out.

c I've run out of money. I just can't afford to go.

d Sorry. She's gone out with her sisters.

e Well, he won't be happy, that's for sure.

f He started out as a drummer.

6 ★★★ **Answer the questions about you.**

1 How often do you go out in a week?

2 Do you know somebody who's good at sorting out problems? How does he/she do it?

3 Do you often buy music that's just come out?

4 How do you find out what songs are cool?

READING

1 REMEMBER AND CHECK **Answer the questions. Then check your answers in the online forum on page 49 of the Student's Book.**

0 What does winning *The X Factor* probably guarantee? *At least one hit album.*

1 What doesn't it guarantee? _____

2 What have Justin Bieber and Lily Allen's careers got in common? _____

3 How did Scooter Brown discover Justin Bieber? _____

4 What is busking? _____

5 Where did Eric Clapton busk before he became famous? _____

2 **Read the article quickly. What is the name of the singer? What are the names of his first two albums? Were they successful?**

_____
_____
_____

A young man dreams of a career in music. He gets a chance to record two albums, but they don't sell. For many years, he lives on very little money. He has no idea that in the meantime his songs have become extremely popular in other countries, and that his fans believe he's dead.

It sounds like the stuff that fairy tales are made of, but it isn't. It's an incredible but true story and this is only the half of it.

Sixto Rodriguez was the son of Mexican immigrants to the US. He released his first album, *Cold Fact*, in 1970, and his second, *Coming from Reality*, a year later. But nobody bought his music, so he had to do all kinds of jobs to survive. Life was hard for him and his family.

In the meantime, his music was becoming a huge success in three countries on the other side of the world: Australia, New Zealand and, in particular, South Africa. There, Rodriguez was a huge star, more popular than the Rolling Stones. But there were rumours that he was dead, and he himself had no idea about the success of his music.

Then, finally, in December 1994, 28 years after he released *Cold Fact,* a young South African fan named Stephen 'Sugar' Segerman and Craig Bartholomew, a journalist, wanted to find out more about Rodriguez. They started a website called The Great Rodriguez Hunt, and had his face put on milk cartons in the US, with the question 'Have you seen this man?'. Rodriguez's daughter saw one and the rest is rock history.

In March 1998, he was invited on a big tour across South Africa. Rodriguez played six concerts all over the country, in stadiums filled with thousands of young people who knew every word to every one of his songs.

In 2012, Swedish film maker Malik Bendjelloul released the documentary film *Searching for Sugar Man*. When the film got a nomination for an Oscar, the director asked Rodriguez to come to the ceremony, but he refused because he feared all the attention would be on him and not the film-makers. The film has helped to make his music successful around the world, but Rodriguez has remained very modest. He's been living in the same simple house in Detroit for 40 years, and he doesn't have a car, a mobile phone or a TV.

3 **Read the article again. Mark the sentences A (right), B (wrong) or C (doesn't say).**

0 Sixto Rodriguez's parents were Mexican and he was born in Detroit, US. `C`

1 Lots of people knew his music in South Africa. ☐

2 His daughter put a picture of him on milk cartons. ☐

3 Twenty-eight years after *Cold Fact*, he played in front of thousands of fans in South Africa. ☐

4 Many people knew the lyrics of his songs. ☐

5 The film about Rodriguez got a nomination for an Oscar, but it didn't win. ☐

4 **When she saw the advert, Rodriguez's daughter called Stephen 'Sugar' Segerman. Use your imagination to write the first six lines of that phone call.**

DAUGHTER Hello, is that Stephen Segerman?

SEGERMAN _____

DAUGHTER _____

SEGERMAN _____

DAUGHTER _____

SEGERMAN _____

DEVELOPING WRITING

A magazine article

1 Read the article quickly. Answer the questions.

0 What's the singer's real name?

Ella Yelich-Amidst

1 Where did she grow up?

2 What do experts think of her?

3 What does the writer think of her?

Young and world famous

A In 2013 a song called 'Royals' made a young singer called Lorde famous all over the world. Lorde (real name Ella Marija Lani Yelich-O'Connor) grew up in New Zealand. She is the daughter of a Croatian father and an Irish mother, and has got a younger brother and two sisters. Her unique talent was discovered when she was 12, and she started writing songs when she was 13.

B Ever since Lorde appeared on TV screens for the first time, critics have been praising her fantastic voice, her feel for the rhythm and the music, and also her lyrics. Her mother, herself a poet, encouraged her to read books from an early age, and that is probably what has made the young singer such a good lyrics writer. She says her love for words has been at least as important as her love for music, and both have helped her enormously to become the star she now is.

C Lorde is very young. She became a star when she was 17, and has had a number of successful songs since then. Among them are 'Royals' and 'Tennis Court', which was released in the UK just after the Wimbledon women's final in 2013.

D I have been fascinated by Lorde's music and her personality since I first saw and heard her in a video clip on the Internet. Her songs make me happy. When I hear 'Royals' on the radio, I turn up the music and sing along. I am sure she will have many more hits.

2 Complete the sentences. Use the correct form of the verbs.

0 She *started* (start) writing songs when she was 13.

1 Ever since Lorde _____ (appear) on TV screens for the first time, experts _____ (praise) her talent.

2 I _____ (be) fascinated by Lorde's music and personality since I first _____ (see) her in a video clip.

3 Look at the sentences in Exercise 2. Find examples of verb forms which refer to …

0 something that happened at a specific time in the past.

She started writing songs when she was 13.

1 something that started in the past, and is still continuing.

2 how long something has been happening.

4 Which paragraph of the text talks about …

0 the artist's history? [A]

1 examples of her songs? ☐

2 what experts say about her? ☐

3 the writer's personal opinion? ☐

5 Plan an article about a writer or a musician alive today. Use the questions and tips to help you.

● Who do you want to write about?

● Find out about the artist's life.

● Find out about the artist's personal situation.

● What do experts think about the artist's success?

● What's your personal opinion?

6 Write a magazine article about a musician or a singer (about 190 words). Use the article and Exercise 5 to help you.

LISTENING

1 🔊20 **Listen to the conversations and answer the questions.**

CONVERSATION 1

0 What do William's friends like that he doesn't?
Listening to music while doing other things.

1 Why can't he listen to music while he's doing something else?

_____

2 When does he like to listen to music?

_____

CONVERSATION 2

3 How does Chloë feel about music?

_____

4 Do her teachers allow her to listen to music during the lessons?

_____

5 How does music make her feel?

_____

CONVERSATION 3

6 Where does Ryan find new music?

_____

7 What are his favourite types of music?

_____

8 Does he listen to music when he works?

_____

DIALOGUE

1 🔊20 **Match the questions and answers. Then listen again and check.**

0 Why's that?   `d`
1 So do you never listen to music? ☐
2 Does it relax you? ☐
3 Could you be without music? ☐
4 Do you dance a lot? ☐
5 When do you listen to that? ☐

a Yeah, it helps me see pictures.
b Not as often as I'd like to.
c Well, when I need to think.
d Because I can't concentrate on both things.
e No, I don't think I could.
f No – I do. I quite like music.

PHRASES FOR FLUENCY

1 **Put the conversation in the correct order.**

☐ EMMA It's The Fall – they're playing in the town hall on Saturday.

☐ EMMA Why don't we invite Gavin to come along?

`1` EMMA Dan, Dan!

☐ EMMA Why not? He loves them.

☐ EMMA Well, if you say so. It's just me and you, then.

☐ EMMA Yes, really. I've already got my tickets. I can't wait! It's going to be the show of the year.

☐ DAN Tell me about it. They're my favourite band. I'm definitely going too.

☐ DAN Gavin? No way.

☐ DAN What's up, Emma?

☐ DAN What?! Really?

☐ DAN Listen, there's no point in trying to change my mind. Gavin and I … well, we just don't like each other. I'd rather not invite him.

2 **Complete the conversations with the expressions in the list.**

if you say so | there's no point in | I can't wait
no way | tell me about it | what's up

0
A Stephen King is the best writer in the world.
B *If you say so* . I prefer Jane Austen.

1
A I've told her again and again that she's wrong.
B _____ talking to her. She just won't listen.

2
A Wow, that lesson was boring.
B _____ . I almost fell asleep twice!

3
A Let's climb that tree.
B _____ . That's far too dangerous.

4
A Hey, Tom. I need to talk to you.
B OK, Julian. _____ ?

5
A I'm so happy it'll be summer soon.
B Me too. _____ to go swimming.

Listening for specific information

1 🔊 **21** Eduardo is thinking about having English lessons. Listen and complete the information.

THE LIMES SCHOOL OF ENGLISH

COURSE A:
Lessons every [0] _Monday_ and [1] _____
Number of lessons per week: [2] _____
Length of lessons: [3] _____ minutes
Cost: [4] £_____ per week

COURSE B:
Lessons every [5] _____ and _____
Number of lessons per week: [6] _____
Length of lessons: [7] _____ minutes
Cost: [8] £_____ per week

Exam guide: completing notes

- Sometimes, in class or in an examination, you have to listen to something and get specific information. It could be, for example, people's names, or numbers, or a time, or dates, or a price, and so on.

- It's important to look carefully at the task before the listening starts.

- Read the questions and instructions carefully. What kind of information does the question ask you to find? A date? A time? A name? A place?

- You don't need to understand everything in the recording. Look at the questions and listen carefully for the answers. It might be frustrating if you don't understand everything, but remember – you only need to identify certain things in order to do the task successfully.

- Look at the listening exercises on this page. What kind of information did you need to do Task 1? And what kind of information do you need for Task 2? It isn't usually possible to be 100 per cent sure about your predictions, though. For example, think about Task 2, answer 7. What kinds of things might a hotel not accept? Children? Credit cards? Pets?

- Remember that you'll probably hear some information that you don't need. For example, in Task 1, you hear the price of each lesson, but you don't have to write it down for the task. Also, you don't need to write down how many lessons there are each day – only how many lessons each week.

- It's possible that the information you want doesn't come in the same order as in the task. There's an example of this in Task 2.

2 🔊 **22** Jean phones a bed and breakfast. Listen and complete the information.

Sea View Bed and Breakfast

- Single room: [0] £ _110_ per night
- Double room: [1] £_____ per night
- All rooms have [2] _____ and [3] _____ .

- Check-in time: [4] _____
- Check-out time: [5] _____
- Car park: [6] £_____ per night
- Sorry, we don't accept [7] _____ .

6 MAKING A DIFFERENCE

GRAMMAR

will (not), may (not), might (not) for prediction SB p.58

1 ★ ☆ ☆ **Match the sentences with the pictures.**

 A
 B
 C
 D
 E
 F

0 Mum won't be happy when she sees her car. `F`

1 Mum will be happy when she sees her car. ☐

2 Don't eat it all. You'll be ill. ☐

3 Don't eat it. It might be poisonous. ☐

4 She may not finish her book tonight. ☐

5 She won't finish her book tonight. ☐

2 ★ ☆ ☆ **Complete the sentences. Use *will* or *won't* and the verbs in the list.**

be | cost | like | believe | get | remember

0 He's grown a lot. He *will be* _____ taller than me soon.

1 Wow! They _____ me when I tell them!

2 I don't know how much this DVD _____ .

3 The cake is for Jill. I'm sure she _____ it.

4 Don't worry. I _____ there as soon as I can.

5 Listen carefully. Otherwise you _____ what I tell you.

3 ★★ ☆ (Circle) **the correct words.**

0 I'm nervous. Mum (might) / won't get angry.

1 Wait there. I *'ll* / *might* be two minutes.

2 I don't know the answer. Who *won't* / *might* know?

3 Both teams are good. I've got no idea who *will* / *won't* win.

4 It's getting late. We *may* / *may not* miss the train.

5 I'll tell you, but you *might* / *won't* believe me.

6 They probably *won't* / *might not* come at all.

4 ★★★ **Write predictions using suitable modal verbs.**

0 there / be / no cars / 20 years from now (certainty)
   There will be no cars 20 years from now.

1 we / visit / the US / next summer (possibility)
   _____

2 I / watch / film / in English / next week (possibility)
   _____

3 they / not see / a match / on Sunday (certainty)
   _____

4 next month / there / be / a lot of rain (possibility)
   _____

5 Jim / go / to university / one day (certainty)
   _____

6 Sally / watch TV / tonight (possibility)
   _____

5 ★★★ **Tick (✓) the predictions in Exercise 4 that are true for you. Change the others so that they are true for you.**

0 ☐ _____
1 ☐ _____
2 ☐ _____
3 ☐ _____
4 ☐ _____
5 ☐ _____
6 ☐ _____

6 ★★★ **Write six sentences about the future of your country. Use *will*, *won't*, *might (not)* and *may (not)*.**

First conditional; *unless* in first conditional sentences `SB p.61`

7 ★☆☆ (Circle) the correct words.

0 If I *see / 'll see* her again, I'll tell her to phone you.

1 We won't go on holiday if Dad *is / will be* still ill.

2 If you *won't / don't* talk about it, nobody will know.

3 *Will / Do* they want to come if they hear about the party?

4 If they don't help, their parents *will be / are* angry.

5 If you think carefully, I'm sure you *find / 'll find* a nice present for her.

6 There won't be many people at the match if the weather *gets / will get* worse.

7 If you *won't / don't* keep in touch with your friends, they'll lose interest in you.

8 ★★☆ Match the sentence halves.

0 I'll take the train   `d`

1 Will they come for lunch   ☐

2 If you don't tell Tracy about the situation,   ☐

3 I won't phone you   ☐

4 If they don't want to come to your party,   ☐

5 She'll only buy the phone   ☐

6 If people hear how much the tickets are,   ☐

7 Unless the teacher gives us really difficult homework,   ☐

a I'll finish it before 7 o'clock.

b you'll have to accept their decision.

c a lot of them won't go.

d unless Dad offers to drive me.

e if it isn't too expensive.

f how will she know?

g unless I change my plans.

h if we invite them?

9 ★★☆ Complete the text. Use the correct form of the verbs in the list.

~~be~~ | not pass | invite | be | go | not let | miss

Dear Diary,

Not a great day today. Had a test in French. Unless I'm totally wrong, the results ⁰ *won't be* very good.
If I ¹_____, I don't know what I'll do. My parents ²_____ me go to the cinema with Bryan tomorrow unless I pass. If I tell Bryan I can't go to the cinema with him, he ³_____ someone else. If he ⁴_____ with someone else, I ⁵_____ a film I'd love to see. But what if I wait and tell my parents later? Well, who knows how they'll react? I think that unless I come up with a brilliant idea, I ⁶_____ in trouble whatever I do. Well, one thing's for sure: next time I'll prepare better for my French test.

10 ★★★ Write first conditional questions. Then match them with the answers.

0 rain / what / you do

    If it rains, what will you do?   `d`

1 watch TV tonight / what / you / watch

_____ ☐

2 what / you / buy / get / birthday money

_____ ☐

3 feel hungry / at break / what / you / eat

_____ ☐

4 what / you / do / not pass / the exam

_____ ☐

5 what / you / do / lose / your phone

_____ ☐

a I'll ask my mum for a new one.

b That won't happen!

c Nothing. I think I'll save the money.

d I'll stay at home.

e I'll watch a film.

f A sandwich or some biscuits.

11 ★★★ Answer four of the questions in Exercise 10 about you.

GET IT RIGHT! 👁

First conditional tenses

Learners sometimes use *will* instead of the present tense in the first conditional.

✓ I will be pleased if they **like** it.

✗ I will be pleased if they ~~will~~ like it.

Correct the following sentences.

0 I'll let you know if we'll be late.

    I'll let you know if we're late.

1 If we have some help, there isn't a problem.

_____

2 I will wear a coat if it will be cold.

_____

3 They'll understand if you'll explain it.

_____

4 Will he go if the meeting will be at 7.00?

_____

5 If it won't rain, they'll have a picnic.

_____

Pronunciation

/f/, /v/ and /b/ consonant sounds

Go to page 119.

VOCABULARY

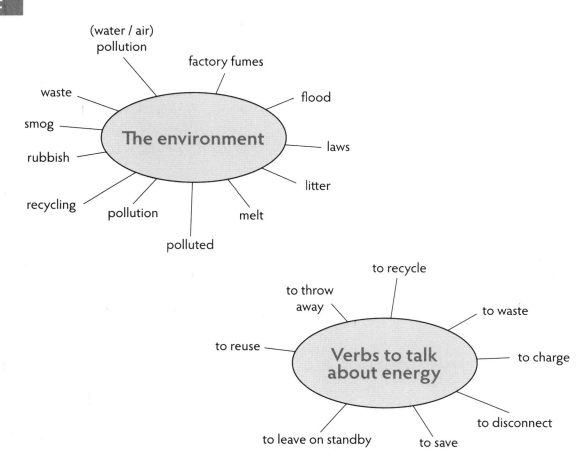

Key words in context

climate change	Experts say **climate change** is responsible for some of the hurricanes.
consequence	If I don't pass this test, the **consequences** will be serious. Dad won't take me to Disneyland!
damage	The fire did a lot of **damage** to the house.
deforestation	**Deforestation** is destroying large areas of tropical rainforest.
endangered species	We have to protect **endangered species** such as the black rhino.
energy	All the **energy** we need to heat the pool comes from the sun.
fear	Scientists **fear** the problems will become bigger over the next few years.
financial	**Financial** interests play a big role in deforestation.
fragile	Be careful how you hold it. It's **fragile** and breaks very easily.
generation	We have to think of the next **generation** and stop pollution.
global warming	Most people agree that **global warming** is making our Earth hotter and is causing problems with our weather.
industry	The financial **industry** in the UK makes more money than the manufacturing industry these days.
landscape	I saw a film about New Mexico and I was fascinated by the **landscape**.
ocean	Is the Atlantic **Ocean** bigger than the Pacific?
organism	The Great Barrier Reef is the only living **organism** you can see from space.
overfishing	Many kinds of fish are disappearing because of **overfishing**.
responsibility	Well, you're the boss, so it's your **responsibility**.
threat	Global warming is a **threat** to our future.
tiny	It's **tiny**. I don't think I've ever seen a bird so small.
tribe	The Amazon rainforest is home to more than 300 **tribes**.

The environment SB p.58

1 ★☆☆ **Write the words under the pictures.**

~~factory fumes~~ | rubbish | flood | litter
pollution | waste | recycling | smog

1 *factory fumes* _____

2 _____

3 _____ , _____ , _____ , _____

2 ★★☆ **Match the sentence halves.**

0	Many people think we need stricter	*g*
1	Plastic bags produce	
2	If global warming continues, many glaciers	
3	Some parts of the world don't get enough rain,	
4	In many of the world's largest cities,	
5	Recycling paper means	
6	This river's water is very clean – it doesn't seem	
7	To help the environment, we should recycle	

a while others get flooded all the time.
b will melt and this will be terrible.
c polluted at all.
d rubbish and we must never produce litter.
e far too much waste.
f smog and factory fumes cause bad air pollution.
g laws to protect the environment.
h we don't need to cut down so many trees.

Verbs to talk about energy SB p.61

3 ★★☆ ⬭**Circle** the correct option: A, B, C or D.

0 If you reuse something,
  A you throw it away.
  B you use it for the last time.
  C you waste a lot of energy.
  ⬭D you use it again.

1 Recycling helps to
  A understand pollution.
  B save energy.
  C throw things away.
  D waste energy.

2 It's better to disconnect electrical appliances
   from their
  A owners.   B smog.
  C power source.   D standby.

3 Certain whales belong to the world's
  A endangered tribes.
  B fragile organisms.
  C endangered species.
  D tiniest organisms.

4 Cutting down too many forests causes
  A deforestation.   B consequences.
  C responsibilities. D financial interests.

5 Experts say that a lot of damage has been done
   to the world's
  A energy.   B fear.
  C pollution.   D oceans.

6 The future of the world is everybody's
  A generation.   B damage.
  C trouble.   D responsibility.

7 Climate change is making the environment
  A tiny.   B fragile.
  C polluted.   D endangered.

4 ★★★ **Answer the questions.**

1 What do you think is the biggest threat to our
   environment and why?
   _____
   _____

2 How do you feel when you see someone throw
   litter on the street?
   _____
   _____

3 Have you ever told somebody not to pollute the
   environment? How did they react?
   _____
   _____

4 What positive examples do you know of people
   caring for the environment?
   _____
   _____

READING

1 REMEMBER AND CHECK **Answer the questions. Then check your answers in the article on page 57 of the Student's Book.**

0 What animals do people kill because they think they have special powers?
The black rhino.

1 Why are rare species of fish more in danger from overfishing than others?

2 How much of the world is covered in forests?

3 Why are people cutting down forests? (two reasons)

4 How long have we already had the problem of rising sea water temperatures?

5 What effects might it have on coastal cities if temperatures rise further?

2 **Read the article quickly. Answer the questions.**

1 Who is the girl in the photo?

2 Where is she from?

3 Where did she give a speech?

3 **Read the article again. Mark the sentences T (true) or F (false). Correct the false information.**

0 Severn was 12 when she managed to speak to the UN Assembly in Brazil. `T`

1 She got the money for the trip to Brazil from some friends at the United Nations. ☐

2 She spoke about a number of serious problems the world was facing. ☐

3 One topic she didn't talk about was the situation of human beings. ☐

4 When she finished, people stood up and clapped. ☐

5 The example of Severn shows that unless you're an adult, you can't make a difference to the world. ☐

4 **Imagine you have the chance to speak to the world leaders. What are you going to speak about and why? Write a short text (50–100 words).**

I am going to speak about …

A young girl who made people listen and made a difference

Let's say that you're 12 years old, you feel strongly about something and you want to talk about it. Perhaps, though, you think that no one wants to hear what you have to say. Well, there are examples of young people who have made the adult world pay attention.

One example is Severn Cullis-Suzuki from Canada. Many years ago, when she was very young, she learned that the United Nations Assembly was going to meet in Brazil in 1992. Severn decided that she wanted not only to go there but also to say something. She started to raise money for the trip and when she was 12, she had enough for the 11,000-kilometre journey.

Severn was sure that she had something to say, and when she made her five-minute speech to the UN Assembly, she tried very hard to make an impact. Severn stood up and talked to the Assembly about a lot of things. She talked about environmental issues like pollution and the hunting of animals to extinction, but she also talked about the situation of children in many parts of the world, poor and starving children in particular. She contrasted them with children in richer countries who have more than they need and throw things away. Severn didn't pretend to have any answers, but her questions were a challenge to the world's leaders – questions about why the adults who run the world don't take more care of it and of the people who live in it.

Many people who heard her speech were crying at the end, and the audience gave her a standing ovation when she finished.

So, the lesson is that your age isn't the important thing. Severn showed that young people can make a difference, providing they're brave enough to believe in themselves. Who knows? Perhaps you could be another Severn.

DEVELOPING WRITING

An article to raise awareness about an environmental issue

1 **Read the extracts. Which of them …**

1 outline a problem? `A` and ☐

2 describe what will happen if nothing is done? ☐ and ☐

3 suggest what to do? ☐ and ☐

A
These attractive birds live near rivers. They eat frogs and other small animals. The species is endangered because the birds cannot find enough food any more. Cities are getting bigger and bigger, and humans destroy their natural habitat.

B
If we don't stop pollution, the temperature will rise further. If the Earth gets hotter, it will have dramatic consequences. If we don't act now, it might be too late.

C
First, we must introduce new laws to stop deforestation. The laws should say that big companies that have earned millions from producing paper have to invest some of their money to save the rainforest.

D
Some people believe that having a wild animal in a cage at home is something special. This is why, every year, thousands of exotic animals die on their way to other countries and continents.

E
First, we need to make sure that there are enough trains and buses so that people can travel to work on public transport. Then we need to let people know what will happen if everybody uses their car all the time.

F
We need to do something now. If the level of the oceans keeps rising, many small islands will be flooded. People and animals will die. This will all happen for sure unless we all change things now.

2 **Complete the sentences from Exercise 1 with linking words.**

0 The species is endangered _because_ they cannot find enough food any more.

1 Some people believe that having a wild animal in a cage at home is something special. _____, every year, thousands of exotic animals die on their way to other countries and continents.

2 This will all happen for sure _____ we all change things now.

3 We need to make sure that there are enough trains and buses _____ that people can travel to work.

4 We need to let people know what will happen _____ everybody uses their car all the time.

- If you want to raise awareness about an environmental issue, you need to structure your text very carefully.

3 **Read the phrases in the list. Which ones are …**

1 a description of a problem?
   Every year, we lose … _____

2 talking about consequences?
   _____

3 a suggested action?
   _____

- If we don't stop now, there will be …
- Unless people begin to change their behaviour, it might be too late.
- In five years' time, most of the animals will …
- Then we have to …
- Forty per cent of the species in that area are in danger.
- The air in big cities is terribly polluted.
- We must introduce new laws to stop …
- Every year, we lose …
- First we need to …
- The species is endangered because …
- We might have bigger problems soon.

4 **Write an article about an environmental issue (about 200 words). If you have already written about a global problem (page 63 of the Student's Book), write about a local problem now. If you have written about a local problem, write about a global issue.**

- Describe the problem.
- Explain what will or might happen if nothing changes.
- Make suggestions to solve it.

LISTENING

1 🔊25 **Listen to the conversations and match them with the pictures.**

 A

 B

Oh! Your birthday! Sorry, I forgot!

 C

2 🔊25 **Listen again and answer the questions.**

CONVERSATION 1

0 Where does Vicky's aunt live?
She lives in the US.

1 What has she invited Vicky to do?

2 What does Vicky invite Henry to do?

CONVERSATION 2

3 What's Isaac planning to do at the weekend?

4 Who's he going to invite?

5 Why isn't Anne so happy about his plans?

CONVERSATION 3

6 What's Oliver going to do on Sunday?

7 Where's he going to do it?

DIALOGUE

1 🔊25 **Match the sentences. Then listen again and check.**

0 She's invited me.	e
1 Are you all right?	
2 Are you sure Mike and Nick are excited too?	
3 I'll be able to see all the drivers up close.	
4 Well, you don't think it's a great idea, do you?	

a Yeah, I'm fantastic. I'm planning something great for the weekend.

b Wow! How come?

c Well, to be honest, no.

d I haven't told them. But I'm sure they'll think it's great.

e I know, and I think that's wonderful.

2 **Complete the phrases with the missing vowels.**

0 Wh*a*t *a* gr*e*a*t id*e*a!

1 Th __ t's __ m __ z __ ng!

2 Th __ t s __ __ nds __ xc __ t __ ng!

3 W __ w!

4 __ h, r __ __ lly?

5 H __ w __ xc __ t __ ng!

6 C __ __ l!

7 __ ncr __ d __ bl __ !

3 **Write two short conversations about people telling their friends some exciting news.**

▰▰▰ TRAIN TO THiNK ▰▰▰

Recognising different text types

1 **Read the extracts and write the text types. Check your answers on page 60 of the Student's Book.**

0 Hi Jane, Gr8 you'll come over to my place on Sunday. Got some cool DVDs. Love, B
Text message

1 Pop in and check out our vegetables – grown by local farmers and brought to you daily by us.

2 A spokesman for SpaceLive said to reporters on Tuesday that the company was thinking of sending plants to the moon.

3 He opened his eyes. He had no idea where he was, but he knew the place was dangerous.

4 Jane, please feed the cat. Food's in the fridge. See you tonight, Mum

5 Monday: another cool day at school. Science project interesting, working with Lisa. Tomorrow photography club.

Help with reading: skimming a text

- When you skim a text, you don't read it word for word. You read it quite quickly to try to understand the main idea.

- Skimming is a useful technique to decide if you want to read a text or not. By skimming a text, you'll get a general idea of what's in it, so you can decide if it makes sense for you to read it in detail. Many people use skimming when they read a newspaper – they only want to read a story in detail if it's something they're interested in, and to decide that, they skim the text first.

Tip: skimming a text

- To skim a longer text, read the title, the first two paragraphs, one or two paragraphs in the middle and the last paragraph (or the last two).
- To skim a shorter text, read the beginning, a little bit from the middle and the ending.
- To skim a paragraph, read the first and the last sentences.
- To skim, move your eyes faster than you would normally do, and don't read every word.
- Photos and other visuals (for example, graphs) may help you to get the main idea of a text too.

1 Skim the paragraph and write what the main idea is. Use the tip to help you.

For most people, watching mega sports events such as the Olympic Games is an enjoyable activity. Millions of people sit in front of their TVs every four years, and countries are very keen to become the hosts of the Games. However, all this fun has consequences for the environment, and they aren't fun at all. Mountains of litter are produced at big sporting events, from plastic bottles to plates, from packaging to food waste and tons of paper. An enormous amount of resources is needed to build the stadiums and the places where athletes, officials and journalists live during the event. And all those thousands of people need to travel from far away. It's no secret that this causes air pollution.

This text is about:

_____

2 Skim the longer text and write what the main idea is. Use the tip to help you.

London Zoo is one of Britain's top attractions and is the world's oldest scientific zoo, founded over 180 years ago. It can be found in the heart of London, in Regent's Park. It is run by the Zoological Society of London.

Although this zoo is located in the middle of the city, it still has plenty of animals to see, including lions, camels, giraffes, penguins, tigers, monkeys and meerkats. In fact, there are 750 different species, making it one of the largest collections of animals in the UK.

The zoo is divided up into many different areas, which are great fun to explore and help make it one of London's most popular tourist attractions.

Gorilla Kingdom
Gorilla Kingdom is home to a colony of Western Lowland gorillas, which live together with other primates.

The African Bird Safari
The African bird house is full of beautiful birds that share the environment with other animals from Africa.

Butterfly Paradise
As visitors walk through this area, they are surrounded by free-flying butterflies from Africa, South-East Asia and Central and South America, seeking out plants on which to feed and rest.

Lions and tigers
London Zoo is home to a family of Asian lions and a pair of Sumatran tigers, and visitors can get very close to the zoo's beautiful but endangered big cats.

Aquarium
The Aquarium is split into three areas and features many exotic and weird fish and a stunning coral reef.

Penguin Beach
Opened in 2011, Penguin Beach is England's biggest penguin pool. It has underwater windows to allow visitors to watch the birds swimming.

There are several places where you can buy food and drink, and souvenirs can be purchased in the gift shop.

London Zoo is located at the north end of Regent's Park, a ten-minute walk through the park from Regent's Park tube station on the Bakerloo line, or a shorter walk from Camden Town tube station on the Northern Line.

This text is about:

_____

CONSOLIDATION

LISTENING

1 🔊26 **Listen to the conversation. Tick (✓) A, B or C.**

1 Who chose the name of the band?
   A Alice ☐
   B Ian ☐
   C Ben ☐

2 What instrument does Ian play in the band?
   A keyboard ☐
   B guitar ☐
   C drums ☐

3 What instrument does Liz play?
   A trumpet ☐
   B saxophone ☐
   C violin ☐

2 🔊26 **Listen again. Answer the questions.**

0 Why is the band called The Green Warriors?
   To show that they care about the environment.

1 What does Ben do in the band?
   _____

2 What do Jessica and Lucy play in the band?
   _____

3 How long has Liz been playing the saxophone?
   _____

4 Where does the band practise?
   _____

GRAMMAR

3 (Circle) **the correct words.**

I've ⁰*worked /(been working)* at the local nature reserve for three months. I spend half my time at the reserve and half my time visiting schools. I've ¹*already visited / been visiting* about 20 schools in the local area. I think it's very important to talk to teenagers. If they ²*don't / won't* learn how to love the environment, there ³*isn't / won't* be much future for our world. One of the projects I've ⁴*worked / been working* on for the last few months is trying to stop the building of a new power station. Unless we ⁵*do / don't do* something to stop it, it ⁶*will / won't* cause serious problems for the local wildlife because they want to build it on an important nesting site for many rare birds. I've ⁷*already written / been writing* about 30 letters to the local politician, but so far he hasn't ⁸*replied / been replying* to me.

4 **Complete the sentences with the correct present perfect simple or continuous form of the verbs in brackets.**

0 Jane Cooper ___*has been*___ (be) a famous writer for a long time.

1 She _____ (write) over thirty novels now.

2 She _____ (write) novels for many years.

3 She _____ (make) a lot of money.

4 Thousands of people _____ (send) her letters.

5 She _____ (reply) to all of them!

6 Since last month, she _____ (think) about her next novel.

7 But she still _____ (not decide) what the new novel will be about.

VOCABULARY

5 **Match the sentence halves.**

0 Marty James started writing *g*
1 He started ☐
2 They played their first ☐
3 The band entered ☐
4 And they won ☐
5 For their prize they got the chance ☐
6 The song was ☐
7 It soon entered ☐
8 Next month the band are going ☐

a a talent show.
b to record a single.
c downloaded over 200,000 times.
d on a national tour.
e gig in the school hall.
f the competition.
g songs when he was 12.
h a band a year later.
i the pop charts.

6 **Complete the words.**

Three simple ways to make a difference.

- ⁰S *ave*_____ your plastic bags and ¹r_____ them next time you go shopping – don't ²t_____ them ³a_____.

- ⁴R_____ your rubbish – sort out the plastic from the paper and the glass.

- ⁵D_____ electronics at night. Don't leave them on ⁶s_____. It just ⁷w_____ power.

DIALOGUE

7 Complete the conversation with the phrases in the list. There is one phrase that you don't need.

~~What a great idea.~~ | So what's the matter? I can't wait. | No way. | If you say so There's no point in | How exciting! I'm just a bit upset. | What's up, Jennie?

JENNIE   Have you heard the news?

ROB   What news?

JENNIE   We're having a school concert to raise money for the Clean Up Our Air campaign.

ROB   ⁰ *What a great idea.*

JENNIE   And our band's playing.

ROB   1 _____

JENNIE   Isn't it? 2 _____

[Two days later]

ROB   3 _____. You don't look very happy.

JENNIE   It's nothing. 4 _____

ROB   5 _____

JENNIE   Remember the school concert I told you about the other day? Well, it's been cancelled.

ROB   6 _____

JENNIE   Yes, it's true. The headmaster decided it wasn't a good idea.

ROB   It's not right. We've got to do something. I'm going to talk to him now.

JENNIE   7 _____ trying to change his mind. It's not happening!

READING

8 Read the article. Mark the sentences T (true) or F (false).

0   'This Is My Dream' was Kashy's first song.   `F`

1   Five years after he wrote 'This Is My Dream', Kashy decided to put it online.   ☐

2   A Hong Kong TV station wanted to use this song to advertise their shows.   ☐

3   Kashy contacted the TV station and asked to perform in Hong Kong.   ☐

4   People in Hong Kong thought Kashy was famous in his home country.   ☐

5   Kashy is now starting to be successful as a musician.   ☐

Kashy Keegan always wanted to be a pop star and spent years trying to make it happen. In 2007, when he was 22, he wrote what he felt would finally be his big hit, a song called 'This Is My Dream', but it never happened. As the years passed, he started to give up on his musical career and found other jobs. In 2012, he decided to upload the song to a music sharing website called Reverbnation. He hoped someone might hear it and like it.

A few months later, he received an email from Universal Music in Hong Kong. They were starting a new TV station and they wanted to use 'This Is My Dream' as the theme tune to one of their shows. Kashy was really excited and made a deal for $5,000 to allow the TV station to use his song.

The TV station invited Kashy to come over to Hong Kong and perform. He accepted the invitations and was met by hundreds of fans. Everyone there thought he was a big star in the UK. He had to try and explain that back home, no one knew who he was. A little later, Kashy was playing the song live on stage to more than 30,000 screaming fans. After the show, he gave lots of interviews and signed hundreds of autographs. The next day, he saw his face in all the local newspapers and the song went to number one in the iTunes charts.

Two days later, Kashy was back in his job in London, but he is flying out to Hong Kong again soon to play his first live shows. His pop dream is finally happening.

WRITING

9 Write a short text (about 120–150 words) about your favourite song. Include this information:

- who the song is by
- when it was first released
- how popular it became
- what the song is about
- why you like it

7 | FUTURE FUN

GRAMMAR
Future forms SB p.68

1 ★☆☆ Complete the rules with *the present simple, the present continuous, be going to* or *will/won't*.

There are four ways to express the future in English.

1 We often use ＿＿＿＿＿＿ to make predictions about the future.
2 We often use ＿＿＿＿＿＿ to talk about future arrangements.
3 We often use ＿＿＿＿＿＿ to talk about fixed future events.
4 We often use ＿＿＿＿＿＿ to talk about future plans and intentions.

2 ★☆☆ Complete the sentences. Use the correct form of the verbs in the list.

~~leave~~ | close | finish | arrive | open | start

1 The train *leaves* London at 12.40 and ＿＿＿＿＿＿ in Manchester at 14.50.

2 The show ＿＿＿＿＿＿ at 21.00 and ＿＿＿＿＿＿ at 23.15.

3 Today is Sunday. Tomorrow the café ＿＿＿＿＿＿ at 8 am and ＿＿＿＿＿＿ at 7 pm.

3 ★★☆ Read the sentences. Circle the correct descriptions.

0 The film starts at 9 o'clock.
prediction / (fixed event)
1 They're meeting on Saturday.
arrangement / fixed event
2 Her plane arrives at 6 am on Tuesday.
fixed event / prediction
3 She's going to study IT at university.
intention / arrangement
4 They're getting married in June.
arrangement / prediction
5 We won't need phones in the future.
intention / prediction
6 I'm going to act in a film one day.
fixed event / intention
7 She'll be very tall when she's older.
arrangement / prediction
8 She's starting her new job next week.
intention / arrangement
9 They'll win the final easily.
arrangement / prediction
10 We're going to have something healthy for dinner.
intention / arrangement

4 ★★★ Complete the sentences. Use the correct form of the verbs in brackets.

0 Grandma ___*will be*___ (be) pleased to see you.
1 Tonight, Jo and I ＿＿＿＿＿＿ (watch) a film at home.
2 He says he ＿＿＿＿＿＿ (be) a film star one day.
3 My exam ＿＿＿＿＿＿ (be) on Friday next week.
4 I've spoken to Callum and we ＿＿＿＿＿＿ (go) to the cinema on Saturday.
5 I think the world ＿＿＿＿＿＿ (end) with a big 'bang'.
6 My cousin ＿＿＿＿＿＿ (get) married in June.
7 Hurry up! The train ＿＿＿＿＿＿ (leave) in five minutes.
8 He isn't a bad player, but he ＿＿＿＿＿＿ (not win) the championship next year.
9 The shop ＿＿＿＿＿＿ (not open) until ten.
10 They're ＿＿＿＿＿＿ (bring out) a new album soon.

Question tags SB p.71

5 ★★☆ **Write the question tags.**

MS WALL	Good afternoon, Megan. Now, you're 18 years old, ⁰ _aren't you?_
MEGAN	No, 19. My birthday was last week.
MS WALL	And you live in Swansea, ¹_____?
MEGAN	Yes, when I'm not at university.
MS WALL	But you didn't go to school in Swansea, ²_____?
MEGAN	No, my parents lived in London then.
MS WALL	I see. Now you're doing a degree in Education, ³_____?
MEGAN	Yes, that's right.
MS WALL	And you can sing, ⁴_____?
MEGAN	Yes, I sing quite well.
MS WALL	But you can't play the guitar, ⁵_____?
MEGAN	No, I'm afraid not.
MS WALL	You've got three sisters, ⁶_____?
MEGAN	Yes, and two brothers.
MS WALL	You helped organise parties for your sisters, ⁷_____?
MEGAN	Yes, and I looked after my friends' kids sometimes.
MS WALL	But you've never had a job before, ⁸_____?
MEGAN	No, but I'd really like this one. I'm sure I'll be good at it.
MS WALL	You'll be able to start next month, ⁹_____?
MEGAN	Yes, of course. Does that mean I've got the job?
MS WALL	Maybe. We'll let you know.

Nor/Neither / So SB p.71

6 ★★☆ (Circle) **the correct words.**

MS WALL	I think Megan did very well in her interview.
MANAGER	⁰(So)/ Nor do I. She answered the questions very clearly. I liked her!
MS WALL	So ¹*do / did* I! She was very impressive.
MANAGER	But I want to see other people.
MS WALL	²*So / Nor* do I. There's another candidate – his name is James. But I haven't read his application form yet.
MANAGER	Neither ³*did / have* I. But that's OK – I can read it now, quickly.
MS WALL	So ⁴*do / can* I. But I need a break first.
MANAGER	So ⁵*am / do* I. Let's get a cup of coffee.

7 ★★★ **Write James's replies.**

MEGAN	I'm trying to get a job for the holidays.
JAMES	⁰ _So am I._
MEGAN	I've just had an interview.
JAMES	¹_____
MEGAN	I was really nervous.
JAMES	²_____
MEGAN	I didn't sleep well the night before.
JAMES	³_____
MEGAN	If I get the job, I'll start next month.
JAMES	⁴_____
MEGAN	But I don't know if I got the job.
JAMES	⁵_____
MEGAN	I don't like waiting for the answer.
JAMES	⁶_____
MEGAN	I won't know the answer until next week.
JAMES	⁷_____
MEGAN	By the way, what job have you applied for?
JAMES	Children's party organiser. And you?

GET IT RIGHT!
Neither / So do I

Learners sometimes do not use *neither* and *so* when they can be used.

✓ Mike will go to the party and **so** will we.
✗ Mike will go to the party and ~~we will go to the party~~.

Tick (✓) the sentences in which the underlined words can be replaced using *neither* or *so*. Rewrite them where possible.

0 I've met Ian and Tim has met him too.
  I've met Ian and so has Tim.

1 My mum likes soap operas, but I don't. ☐
_____

2 He was there and she was there too. ☐
_____

3 I can't go to the party and Joe can't go. ☐
_____

4 We speak French, but our parents don't. ☐
_____

5 I don't eat meat and he doesn't eat it. ☐
_____

Pronunciation
Intonation in question tags
Go to page 120. 🔊

VOCABULARY

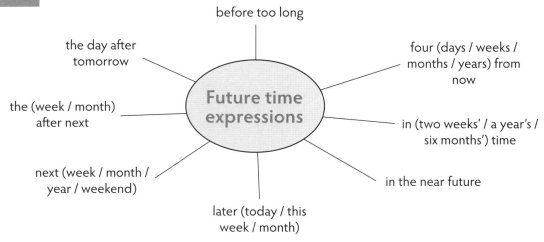

before too long

the day after tomorrow

four (days / weeks / months / years) from now

the (week / month) after next

Future time expressions

in (two weeks' / a year's / six months') time

next (week / month / year / weekend)

in the near future

later (today / this week / month)

Arranging a party

to choose a theme

to hire a DJ

to decorate the room

to send out invitations

to draw up a guest list

to pay a deposit

to get permission

to organise the food

about

about (10 o'clock / half an hour)
about to (go home)
What about you?
sorry about (that)
forget about (it)
think about (it)

Key words in context

poverty	Millions of people around the world live in **poverty**, without enough money to live.
publicity	There's been a lot of **publicity** about her new film in the newspapers.
robot	Soon there will be **robots** that can speak like people.
technology	In the next 30 years, there will be amazing advances in **technology**.
transplant	He was very lucky – he got a heart **transplant** and so he's still alive.
venue	There's a new club in town that's a great **venue** for music and parties.

Future time expressions SB p.68

1 ★☆☆ **Put the words in order to make future time expressions.**

0 too / before / long   *before too long*
1 the / next / week / after   _____
2 tomorrow / the / after / day   _____
3 near / the / future / in   _____
4 now / weeks / from / three   _____
5 time / in / years' / two   _____
6 this / later / month   _____

2 ★★☆ **Answer the questions.**

0 What day is it the day after tomorrow?
   The day after tomorrow is Thursday.
1 Where do you think you'll be in ten years' time?
   _____
2 What do you think will happen later this year?
   _____
3 Do you think you will go abroad in the near future?
   _____
4 Do you think you'll have a car before too long?
   _____
5 What do you think you'll be doing five years from now?
   _____

3 ★★☆ (Circle) **the correct words.**

0 Some scientists think we will put men on Mars *the day after tomorrow /(in the near future.)*
1 Joseph is 14 years old, so he'll be able to drive a car *in a few years' time / a week from now.*
2 My computer is really slow. I'll probably get a new one *before too long / in four years' time.*
3 Natalie is in Rome this week, and she's going to Paris *later this month / in a few hours' time.*
4 The date today is the 1st of December. New Year's Day will be *in a month's time / the week after next.*
5 Julie is on holiday next week, but she'll be back at work *in two days' time / the week after next.*
6 It's December. Paul was born in June, so his next birthday is *in six months' time / in a day's time.*
7 Today is Tuesday. Sue is taking her driving test on Thursday. That's *later this year / in two days' time.*

Arranging a party SB p.71

4 ★★☆ **Megan got the job as a children's party organiser. Complete the phone conversation with the words in the list.**

~~permission~~ | hire | theme | deposit | organise
invitations | room | food | guests

MUM Hello, Megan. How's the job going?
MEGAN I'm working on a party for a boy who's going to be five in two weeks' time.
MUM What have you got to do?
MEGAN Well, it's in the community centre, so I have to get [0] *permission* . Then we choose a [1]_____ – Spider-Man or something – and I find out what [2]_____ the kids want.
MUM Pizzas, probably! Do you have to [3]_____ a cake?
MEGAN Yes. And the parents draw up a list of [4]_____ – all the boy's friends – and I send [5]_____ .
MUM And entertainment?
MEGAN Yes, they want to [6]_____ a clown, so I have to pay a [7]_____ .
MUM It sounds like a lot of work.
MEGAN Yes, it is. But I love it. I enjoy decorating the [8]_____ , but the best part is seeing the kids having fun.

WordWise SB p.73
Phrases with *about*

5 ★★☆ **Complete the conversations with *about* and the words in the list.**

~~six~~ | them | sorry | 75
forget | you | think | to

0 A So, cinema this evening?
   B Yes, OK. I'll see you at *about six* o'clock.
1 A So, will you come with us?
   B I'm not sure, but I'll _____ it.
2 A Hey! You're late!
   B Yes, I'm really _____ that.
3 A He looks really old.
   B Yes, I think he's _____ .
4 A Everyone's going, Sue. What _____?
   B No, I don't want to go, thanks.
5 A What's wrong? Is your homework hard?
   B It's really hard! I'm _____ go crazy!
6 A I'm so sorry I was late yesterday.
   B No problem. Just _____ it, OK?
7 A I need help with my project on the Tudors.
   B Sorry – I don't know anything _____ .

READING

1 REMEMBER AND CHECK Mark the sentences T (true) or F (false). Then check your answers in the article on page 67 of the Student's Book.

0 Titan Moon is the name of a hotel on the moon. `T`

1 Mira Xin is the billionaire woman who owns Titan Moon. ☐

2 Star Client is a robot that's in a new film. ☐

3 A film has been made with robots because human actors want too much money. ☐

4 Shirley Williams is a boxer. ☐

5 She has a new hand after a transplant. ☐

6 It is possible now (in 2042) to send 3D images of yourself around the world. ☐

7 Full-body transportation is still a dream. ☐

2 Read the magazine article. Then match the paragraphs A–D with the answers 1–4.

1 Never. ☐

2 In about twenty years' time, perhaps. ☐

3 Only in about a hundred years' time. `A`

4 Not while I'm still living. ☐

3 Read the article again. Answer the questions.

0 What are the two main problems with trying to live on the moon?
   There is very little oxygen on the moon and there isn't any animal or plant life.

1 Why does Dr Morrison say 'Sorry!' at the end of her answer to question B?
   _____
   _____

2 What are the two main problems with trying to live under the sea?
   _____
   _____

3 Why don't people want to take part in experiments instead of animals?
   _____
   _____

Will we ever ... ?

Many people have questions about the future – will we ever do X, or Y, or Z? In this week's magazine, Dr Jean Morrison answers some of your questions.

A Will people ever live on the moon?
Angie, London

Not in the near future. There are real problems – the big one is that people need oxygen to stay alive and the moon has very little. And there's no animal or plant life on the moon, so what will we do about food? I think one thing is for sure – it won't be before the next century! And the number of people living there will be quite small.

B Will we ever be able to travel through time?
Paul, Cambridge

Well, people are fascinated by the idea of time travel. But that doesn't mean it'll ever be possible. I'd love to be able to go into the past or the future! But I'm sure we'll never be able to. So my answer to this is no, no chance! (Sorry!)

C Will there ever be cities under the sea?
Anthea, Chester

A lot of people are working on this. But there are lots of problems. One is that people need sunlight, and there isn't much sunlight 100 metres under the sea! And another is pressure – how can we build walls that are thick enough to keep the water out? And where will the energy come from? Personally, I don't think we'll see underwater cities in my lifetime. And to be honest, I'd hate to live under the sea and not see the sun!

D Will scientists ever stop using animals for experiments?
Max, Liverpool

I hope so. The problem is that people don't like using animals to test new medicines and drugs, but they don't really want to use human beings because nobody knows for sure what will happen to the people in the experiment. Some people predict that human beings will replace animals more and more in the next 10 to 20 years. All animal lovers hope they're right. And so do I.

DEVELOPING WRITING

An invitation

1 Read the invitation and answer the questions.

INVITATION

It's party time, everyone! Believe it or not,
I'm going to be 15 next month, so please come
to my party and help me to celebrate!

Date: Saturday 16th July

Time: From 8 until late!

Venue: The Mill Room at the Grove Street Youth Club

All you have to bring is yourself (beautifully dressed,
of course!)

Love from,
Jenna

RSVP to jennahall58@gmail.com

1 What day and time is the party?

_____

2 Where is the party?

_____

3 What do people have to bring?

_____

2 Read the replies to the invitation in Exercise 1 and answer the questions.

1 Who's going to the party?

_____

2 Who isn't going and why not?

_____

3 Read the phrases. Circle Y (saying yes), N (saying no) or T (saying thanks).

0	I'm afraid I can't be there.	Y / (N) / T
1	Count me in.	Y / N / T
2	Thanks for inviting me.	Y / N / T
3	See you there / then.	Y / N / T
4	I'm so sorry, but …	Y / N / T
5	I'll be there.	Y / N / T
6	I was so happy to get your invitation.	Y / N / T

4 Read the replies in Exercise 2 again. Put the functions in order.

1 Susanna's reply

A apologise ☐

B say thank you ☐ 1

C suggest another meeting ☐

D say no and give a reason ☐

2 Jeremy's reply

A talk about meeting ☐

B say thank you ☐

C say yes ☐

5 Read the invitation. Write two replies, one to accept and one to refuse (about 50–60 words each). Use the language and functions in Exercises 3 and 4 to help you.

⊖ ◻ ✕

Hi!

Listen, I've just passed my big exams and next Sunday night we're going to have a party at my place to celebrate. I hope you can come. It's at 6 o'clock at my house. Please tell me if you can come, OK? Send me an email.

Hope to see you!

Best,

Graham

⊖ ◻ ✕ **To:** Jennahall58@gmail.com **A**

Hi Jenna,

Wow – another birthday! Congratulations and I'm sure your party is going to be just fantastic!

Thanks for inviting me, but I'm afraid I can't be there. My mum and dad have already booked our holiday and we're going to Spain the night before your party! Can you believe it?

I'm so sorry, but have a wonderful time, OK? And maybe we can have our own celebration when I'm back from holiday – how about it?

Lots of love,

Susanna

⊖ ◻ ✕ **To:** Jennahall58@gmail.com **B**

Hey Jenna,

I was so happy to get your invitation! It's hard to believe that you're going to be 15!

Please count me in. I'll be there. How could I possibly not be? You know that parties aren't the same without me!

I'm looking forward to being with you on the 16th. Are you sure I can't bring anything?

See you then if not before.

Hugs,

Jeremy

LISTENING

1 🔊28 **Listen to the conversations and answer the questions.**

CONVERSATION 1

0 Whose family has plans for a summer holiday – the boy's or the girl's?
    The boy's

1 Does the boy like camping?
    _____

2 Does the girl like camping?
    _____

3 Where is the girl's family going camping?
    _____

4 Who can't talk to their parents – the boy, the girl, or both of them?
    _____

CONVERSATION 2

5 Why doesn't the girl know about her summer plans?
    _____

6 Does the girl like being on a beach?
    _____

7 Does the boy like being on a beach?
    _____

8 What's the weather like while they're talking?
    _____

9 When was the last time the girl went to a beach?
    _____

CONVERSATION 3

10 Who doesn't like summer holidays – the boy or the girl?
    _____

11 What are the three best things for the boy about the summer holidays?
    _____

12 What is the girl going to do in the holidays?
    _____

13 What time does the boy want to get up in the holidays?
    _____

14 Who can stay up until midnight watching TV – the boy, the girl or neither of them?
    _____

15 What does the boy offer to help the girl with?
    _____

DIALOGUE

1 🔊28 **Match the statements with the replies. Then listen again and check.**

0 I think we're going on holiday somewhere.   [e]

1 I really don't like camping.   [ ]

2 Sometimes I just can't talk to my parents.   [ ]

3 I just love being on a beach!   [ ]

4 My parents don't let me do that.   [ ]

a Oh, so do I.

b Neither can I.

c Well, neither do mine.

d Nor do I.

e So are we.

PHRASES FOR FLUENCY

1 **Put the conversation in the correct order.**

[ ] GREG Lucky you! I think Lucy's a really nice girl.

[ ] GREG In other words, you haven't studied for it! Wow! You know, I spent five hours last night studying.

[ ] GREG No, I don't think so. There's nothing wrong with studying.

[1] GREG Hey, Joe. Have you heard? There isn't going to be a test tomorrow.

[ ] GREG Yes, that's a good plan – she loves films!

[ ] JOE So do I. I think I'll take her to the cinema. What do you reckon?

[ ] JOE Five hours? That's a shame. I think you wasted your time.

[ ] JOE Thank goodness! I was worried about that test because I really wasn't ready for it.

[ ] JOE Maybe not. Well, look, I've got to go. I'm taking Lucy out tonight.

2 **Complete the conversations with the expressions in the list.**

~~thank goodness~~ | lucky you | in other words
What do you reckon | There's nothing wrong with
that's a shame

1 A I had an accident yesterday. But I wasn't hurt –
       thank goodness!
    B Well, _____! The last time I had an accident, I broke my arm!

2 A Thanks for the invitation. But I've got another party that night.
    B So, _____, you can't come? Well, _____ – I really wanted you to be there!

3 A I think my hair looks terrible. _____?
    B No, it looks fine. _____ it, honestly!

Reading part 1

1 Read the texts. (Circle) the correct option: A, B or C.

0 A The game this weekend is cancelled.
    (B) John doesn't have Ben's contact details.
    C John doesn't want Ben to play.

1 A You have to like rock to be in the band.
    B You must have experience.
    C The band need someone to play the band's drums.

2 The school wants parents to …
    A drive more carefully.
    B stop dropping off children at the gates.
    C encourage their children to walk to school.

0

> Liam, just to let you know that Saturday's game is now at 3 pm. Any chance you can let Ben know?
> Best, John

1
Wanted
Drummer for rock band.
Must have own drums.
No beginners. Audition
Tuesday after school in
dining room.

2 Last week one of our students was nearly knocked over outside the school gates. If you drive your children to school, can we ask you to drop them off in the car park?

Exam guide: understanding short texts

- In this part of the test you read some very short texts and have to choose the correct answer (A, B or C). The texts could be messages, instructions, signs, postcards, notices, emails, labelling on foods, etc.
- Think about where you might see each text. There might be a visual clue to help you (a TV screen, for example).

- Read each text carefully to get the general meaning.
- Look at each of the options and try to match them up with the information in the text.
- If you can identify false information in any of the options, then eliminate these options.
- When you've made your final choice, read the text again, followed immediately by the option you've chosen, for one final check.

---

2 Read the texts. (Circle) the correct option: A, B or C.

0
Chester Zoo
Children must be accompanied by an adult at all times.

1 There are only two places left on Sunday's coach trip to York. Anyone interested contact Miss Higgins. Anyone who hasn't paid, please do so at the school office before Friday afternoon.

2
Buy one, get one free.

3 Ben – have you finished that book I lent you? It's my sister's and she wants it back – Joe

4
This building is protected by guard dogs and CCTV cameras.

0 A Some parts of the zoo are closed to children.
    B Children can't visit the zoo.
    (C) Someone over 18 needs to stay with any child at the zoo.

1 A The school trip is now completely full.
    B Miss Higgins is accepting money now.
    C You have until the end of the school week to pay for the trip.

2 A If you buy two chocolate bars, you only pay for one.
    B The chocolate is half price.
    C It's cheaper to buy two bars of chocolate than one.

3 What does Joe want Ben to do?
    A return his sister's book
    B return his book
    C lend him a book

4 A Don't enter this building if you aren't invited.
    B No one is allowed in here.
    C This building has a good alarm system.

8 | SCIENCE COUNTS

GRAMMAR

Past simple vs. past continuous (review) SB p.76

1 ★☆☆ **Look at the picture. Complete the sentences with the past continuous form of the verbs in the list.**

~~send~~ | look | play | read | draw | sleep

When the teacher came into the classroom, …

0 Harry _was sending_ a text message.

1 Chloë _____ a picture on the board.

2 Jessica and Sophie _____ a magazine.

3 Steve _____.

4 Sarah _____ out of the window.

5 Mark and Graham _____ football.

2 ★★☆ (Circle) **the correct words.**

0 I *did* / (*was doing*) some shopping when I (*met*) / *was meeting* my friend Sally.

1 When we *got* / *were getting* to the party, everyone *danced* / *was dancing*.

2 It *rained* / *was raining*, so we *decided* / *were deciding* to stay at home.

3 While we *walked* / *were walking* in the park, it *started* / *was starting* to rain.

4 I *fell* / *was falling* asleep while we *watched* / *were watching* a film on TV.

5 He *didn't answer* / *wasn't answering* the phone because he *listened* / *was listening* to music with headphones.

3 ★★★ **Complete the text with the correct past tense form of the verbs.**

Peter and Terry [0] _were sitting_ (sit) in a café. They [1]_____ (not look) out of the window – they [2]_____ (talk). Just then, the waitress [3]_____ (scream) and [4]_____ (drop) the boys' coffee on the floor. When they [5]_____ (look) round, she [6]_____ (look) out to the street. They [7]_____ (look) out too and saw a young man who [8]_____ (get) out of a big car. The waitress [9]_____ (run) outside and [10]_____ (go) up to him. She [11]_____ (hold) a piece of paper. When the waitress [12]_____ (come) back into the café, she [13]_____ (smile). She had her favourite singer's autograph, but Peter and Terry still didn't have any coffee.

used to SB p.77

4 ★★☆ **Complete the conversation with the correct forms of *used to* and the verbs in the list.**

~~listen~~ | listen | play | buy | eat | wear | write | have

JOSEPH   When you were young, did you have TV?

GRANDDAD No, we [0] _used to listen_ to the radio.

JOSEPH   [1]_____ with your friends?

GRANDDAD Yes, we played football, but we didn't have skateboards, just simple skates.

JOSEPH   What about shopping?

GRANDDAD My mother [2]_____ food in small shops, not in supermarkets. She always had to cook for us. We [3]_____ fast food.

JOSEPH   What, no burgers?! [4]_____ to music?

GRANDDAD Of course. We had a record player.

JOSEPH   What was school like?

GRANDDAD Well, we [5]_____ a uniform. And we [6]_____ everything in our notebooks – no computers then. But we [7]_____ a lot of fun. Why all these questions?

JOSEPH   I'm doing a History project.

GRANDDAD Ah, OK. I guess I'm part of history now!

Second conditional `SB p.79`

5 ★☆☆ **Match the sentence halves.**

0 If I knew Hannah's new phone number, `e`

1 If my computer was working, ☐

2 I would walk to the shopping centre ☐

3 Mum would take me in the car ☐

4 I would buy some new jeans ☐

5 If I went to the shopping centre, ☐

a if it wasn't raining.

b if I asked her nicely.

c I would send her an email.

d I would probably meet some of my friends.

e I would phone her.

f if I had more money.

6 ★★☆ (Circle) **the correct words.**

ALAN What ⁰*did / (would)* you do if you ⁰*(were) / would be* alone in a strange city?

BELLE I ¹*didn't / wouldn't* go out. If I ²*went / would go* out alone, I ³*was / would be* scared of getting lost.

ALAN But what ⁴*did / would* happen if you ⁵*got / would get* lost?

BELLE If I ⁶*got / would get* lost, I ⁷*started / would start* to panic.

ALAN ⁸*Did / Would* you ask a stranger for help?

BELLE No way! I ⁹*phoned / would phone* someone.

ALAN I ¹⁰*didn't / wouldn't* be worried if I ¹¹*got / would get* lost. I think it ¹²*was / would be* fun!

7 ★★★ **Complete the sentences so they are true for you.**

0 If I met a famous singer, *I would ask for an autograph.*

1 If I could visit any place in the world, I _____

2 I would be very happy if _____

3 It would be really bad if _____

4 My home town would be more interesting if _____

5 If I didn't live here, I _____

6 If I didn't have to go to school, I _____

7 The world would be better if _____

I wish `SB p.79`

8 ★★☆ **Look at the pictures. Complete the sentences with the correct conditional form and the words in the list.**

~~dance~~ | astronaut | new | curly | stronger | sing

0 I wish *I could dance.*   1 I wish _____

2 I wish _____   3 I wish _____

4 I wish _____   5 I wish _____

GET IT RIGHT!

wish vs. *hope*

Learners sometimes overuse *I wish* where *I hope* is needed.

✓ *I **hope** you will be with me next time.*

✗ *I **wish** you will be with me next time.*

Complete the sentences with *wish* or *hope*.

0 I ___*wish*___ I could be there too, but I have to visit my cousin.

1 I _____ you have a good time in Spain.

2 I _____ I could go there for my birthday.

3 I _____ the weather here was as nice as it is where you are.

4 I _____ things go well for you in your new town.

5 I'm going to get this finished by five – well, I _____ I can, anyway.

VOCABULARY

Word list

Direction and movement

around

away from

towards

backwards

forwards

down

up

up and down

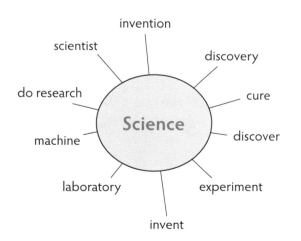

invention
scientist
discovery
do research
cure
Science
machine
discover
laboratory
experiment
invent

Key words in context

achievement	I won the race and for me, that was a great **achievement**.
basic	I'm not very good on the computer, but I can do the **basic** things.
enormous	That house has got twelve bedrooms – it's **enormous**.
identify	They worked hard to try and **identify** the causes of the illness.
malaria	Some mosquitoes carry **malaria**.
pill	He took three **pills** to try to get rid of the pain.
pollute	The dirt from the factory is **polluting** the river.
prevent	They have put traffic lights there to try to **prevent** accidents.
structure	They learned about the **structure** of the atom.
tool	My dad's got lots of **tools** in the garage for fixing his car and things.
treat	He's very unhappy, so please **treat** him nicely.

Direction and movement   SB p.76

1 ★☆☆ **Look at the picture. Complete the sentences with the words in the list.**

~~around~~ | backwards | up | away from
down | towards | up and down | forwards

0 There's a snake. It's moving ___around___ a tree.

1 There's a lion. It's going slowly _____ a white rabbit.

2 There's a small white mouse. It's running _____ the tree.

3 There's a large black mouse. It's running _____ the tree.

4 There's a cat. It's running _____ a dog.

5 There's a kangaroo. It's jumping _____ .

6 There's a monkey. It's swinging _____ and _____ on a rope.

2 ★★☆ **Complete the sentences with direction and movement phrases.**

0 Two boys are playing in the lift. They've already gone _up and down_ six times.

1 It's difficult to walk _____ because you can't see where you're going.

2 I was scared when I saw the tiger coming _____ me.

3 I think he was angry with me because he just turned round and walked _____ me, and out of the door.

4 The children were really excited. They were running _____ the room and shouting.

5 It took two hours to get into the exhibition. The queue moved _____ very slowly.

Science   SB p.79

3 ★★☆ **Use the clues 1–8 to complete the puzzle. What's the mystery word?**

	⁰R	E	S	E	A	R	C	H	
1									
			2						
3									
4									
5									
6									
			7						
8									

0 I'm going to do some _research_ for my science project at school.

1 Some people are trying to _____ a way to build cities under the sea.

2 Did Edison _____ the telephone, or was it someone else?

3 Maybe one day they'll find a _____ for every disease – but perhaps not!

4 Some jobs can't be done by a _____ – they have to be done by people.

5 I think the lift was a very important _____ . It changed buildings completely.

6 Today we did an _____ with electricity.

7 What do you think is the most important scientific _____ of all time?

8 Our school's got a _____ , where we have our science class.

4 ★★☆ **Match the sentence halves to make a paragraph.**

0 My brother loves   [f]
1 He likes to think the kitchen is   [ ]
2 He's done a lot of   [ ]
3 He looks on the Internet to   [ ]
4 Sometimes he just   [ ]
5 He'd like to make   [ ]
6 He thinks he's a sort of   [ ]
7 I wish he could find   [ ]

a discover new ways to make sandwiches.
b research into how to make sandwiches.
c a machine for putting butter on bread.
d food scientist, in fact.
e a cure for my stomach ache.
f doing experiments in the kitchen.
g his laboratory.
h invents his own.

READING

1 REMEMBER AND CHECK Correct the underlined words. Then check your answers in the text on page 75 of the Student's Book.

0 Isaac Newton was walking around in his <u>father's</u> garden.   *mother's*

1 He sat near a tree and an <u>orange</u> fell out of the tree.   _____

2 Newton then got <u>the book</u> about gravity.   _____

3 Archimedes was an old <u>Italian</u> man.   _____

4 One day he got an idea when he was in the <u>shower</u>.   _____

5 He saw how the <u>amount</u> of water changed when he moved.   _____

6 Newton saw that gravity also has an effect on the <u>sun</u>.   _____

7 Archimedes and Newton's discoveries were not complete <u>mistakes</u>.   _____

2 Read the article. Tick (✓) the best title.

1 Films about science in the 20th century ☐

2 'Mad scientists' in books and films ☐

3 Scientists in horror films ☐

4 From *Frankenstein* to *The Fly* ☐

Scientists haven't always been seen as very positive figures. In fact, the idea of the 'mad scientist' has been around for a very long time, and it appears in books and films to this day.

Back in the 19th century, Mary Shelley wrote a story about a scientist called Frankenstein who did an experiment in his laboratory because he wanted to show that he could create life from dead things. He takes bits of dead people and he creates … a monster, of course, that starts to kill people. The Frankenstein story has produced hundreds of film versions – mostly horror films, although there have been one or two comedy ones.

This is the idea of science as something really quite dangerous. Things can – and probably will – go wrong because the scientists don't really know what they're doing. Another example is the film *The Fly*, which was made in 1958 and again in 1986. Here, a scientist wants to

do an experiment on transportation, but it goes wrong when a fly enters the transportation machine with him. He creates a man with parts of a fly's body, and a fly with parts of a man's body. The slogan of the film was *Be afraid. Be very afraid!*

The idea of the 'mad scientist' was especially strong in films in the second half of the 20th century. A survey was done of more than 1,000 horror films from the 1930s to the 1980s.

In 30% of the films, a 'mad scientist' was the bad guy; in 39% of the films, an enormous danger was created by scientific research that went wrong; and the scientist was the hero in only 11% of them.

Sometimes the scientist isn't the bad guy – he's still a bit crazy, but not dangerous. Take Doc in *Back to the Future*, who turns a car into a machine that can travel in time. With his crazy white hair (just like Einstein) and big eyes, he's the genius who makes mistakes but tries hard and is always nice in the end. And in the TV comedy *The Big Bang Theory*, the scientists are nerds but certainly not dangerous.

But the 'mad scientist' idea never goes away altogether. In the 2008 cartoon *Igor*, there's a whole country (called Malaria) that's run by evil scientists. And in the film, the hero, Igor, builds a person from bits and pieces of other people – and there we are, right back to Frankenstein again!

3 Read the article again. Mark the sentences T (true), F (false) or DS (the text doesn't say).

0 The idea of 'mad scientists' isn't a new one.   T

1 All the films about Frankenstein have been horror films.   ☐

2 The film *The Fly* has been made twice.   ☐

3 People were very afraid when they saw *The Fly*.   ☐

4 A survey was done of all the horror films from 1930 to 1980.   ☐

5 Einstein had big eyes.   ☐

6 In *Back to the Future*, Doc doesn't get everything right.   ☐

7 In the cartoon, Igor builds a monster who kills people.   ☐

4 Think of another film or TV programme with scientists in it. Are they shown as good or bad? Write a short text (about 50–100 words).

Pronunciation

The /juː/ sound

Go to page 120. 🔊

DEVELOPING WRITING

How technology changes people's lives

1 Match the texts with the life-changing inventions in the list. There are three that you don't need.

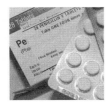
penicillin

the aeroplane

the car

the lift

the syringe

the wheel

A _____

I think it's very hard to imagine what life would be like without [?]. Life in the country might not be too different, but in cities it certainly would be.

Before we had [?], people had to walk a lot more than they do now – up and down, of course, and carrying lots of things. Without it, we wouldn't have towers and really tall buildings like you see in every city in the world. How would you carry all your shopping to your home if you had to walk up to the fifth floor? And it wouldn't be easy to build places like airports, either. How would people go up and down inside with all their heavy suitcases?

I think [?] is one of the most important inventions of all time.

B _____

Can you imagine what things would be like if [?] didn't exist? Everyone's life would be harder. The work of doctors and hospitals would be a lot more difficult, too.

I read once that the discovery of [?] was a kind of accident. Almost a hundred years ago, a scientist in Britain found something surprising in his laboratory and other people discovered how to turn it into this really, really important medicine. It helps people who are sick from many different things, and it's used all over the world.

A long time ago, people didn't use to have [?]. Now life is much better because we've got it.

C _____

I think [?] has changed people's lives a lot – and not always in a good way.

Now that we've got it, people feel freer and they can go to a lot of places much more easily. It used to be very expensive, but prices have gone down a lot in the last twenty or thirty years.

If we didn't have [?], things like the food we eat in many countries would be different. Because of [?], now you can get fish, fruit or other things from one country to another in a very short time – a day or less. So in Britain, for example, we can have fresh pineapple for breakfast, and that used to be impossible.

But [?] makes a lot of noise and creates pollution. Maybe things would be better without fresh pineapple or holidays in faraway countries.

2 Read the text again. Find examples of …

1 the second conditional: *things would be very different,* _____
_____

2 used to: *people didn't use to have it,* _____

3 comparatives: *more difficult,* _____
_____

3 Write a short text about an invention or discovery that you think is really important (100–150 words).

- Choose what to write about – maybe one of the other things in Exercise 1? Or the mobile phone? The computer? The camera?
- What can you can say about how life used to be before we had this thing?
- What can you say about what life would be like if we still didn't have it?
- What comparisons can you make?

You can try to write your text without saying what you're writing about. Then give your text to a partner. Can they say what your text is about?

LISTENING

1 ◀)) 31 Listen to two conversations. Match them with the correct picture.

 A

 B

 C

 D

2 ◀)) 31 Listen again and answer the questions.

CONVERSATION 1

0 Whose vase did the girl's brother break?   *He broke his friend's mother's vase.*

1 Who did her brother tell about the broken vase?

2 Why would John perhaps not do the same thing?

CONVERSATION 2

3 Why is the girl so happy?

4 Why isn't the boy very enthusiastic?

5 What would happen if someone said, 'It wasn't a goal'?

DIALOGUE

1 Put the conversations in the correct order.

CONVERSATION 1

- [ ] A www.helpyourenglish.net
- [ ] A I know – but I'm much better now! I used to spend hours studying at home – but then I found a great website.
- [1] A Hey, look! I got 79 per cent in the English test.
- [ ] A Why not?
- [ ] B Oh, yes – I know that one. I used to use it a lot. But not any more.
- [ ] B Because I found a better one. And look – I got 92 per cent in the English test!
- [ ] B Seventy-nine per cent? That's great. But you used to be really bad at English.
- [ ] B Oh, yes? What's it called?

CONVERSATION 2

- [ ] A So he doesn't work there any more?
- [1] A I can't go out tonight. I'm working on a presentation about experiments on animals.
- [ ] A Your dad? Why?
- [ ] A Your dad worked in a laboratory like that?
- [ ] B Because he used to work in a laboratory where they tested things on animals.
- [ ] B No, he left after a year. Now he works in a pet shop – he loves it!
- [ ] B Yes, but he hated it. He used to come home really angry. We used to keep very quiet!
- [ ] B Animal testing? Really? You should talk to my dad, then.

◼◼ TRAIN TO THiNK ◼◼

Using criteria

1 Look at the inventions on page 77 again. Some people were asked which they think is the best. Match the beginnings and ends of their answers.

0 It's penicillin, because — *e*

1 It's the plane, because — [ ]

2 It's the car, because — [ ]

3 It's the lift, because — [ ]

4 It's the syringe, because — [ ]

5 It's the wheel, because — [ ]

a you can't give some medicines without it.

b people don't have to use stairs any more.

c other things (like cars) depend on it.

d you don't have to walk or use bicycles or horses any more.

e it helps people who have bad illnesses.

f it lets people travel all over the world.

2 Write three inventions or discoveries that you think may be the best. Say why.

1 It's _____ , because _____

2 It's _____ , because _____

3 It's _____ , because _____

Help with reading: scanning a text

- When you scan a text, you look for specific information – a price, a year, a place, a name, etc. – without trying to read the whole text or understand what it's all about. When you scan a text, it's important that you move your eyes quickly down the page.

- Scanning is a very useful technique if you have little time available and only need certain precise information from a text.

Tip: scanning a text

- To scan a text successfully, you first of all need to know exactly what you're looking for. If, for example, you're reading a text about an invention and want to find out when it's from, you know that the answer will be a year, so you're looking for a number.

- Then try to find quickly where in the text the information can be found. Don't read the text word for word – just move your eyes quickly vertically (up and down) and horizontally (across) the page until you've found the place in the text where the information is.

- Once you've found the place, you need to make sure the information you're taking from the text is accurate. Don't go too fast now – it's better to check twice if you've really found the information you've been looking for.

1 **Look at the grid to see what information is missing. Scan the text for the missing information and complete the grid.**

JAMES WATT:

Year of birth: 0 __1736__	Place of birth: 1_____
Year he started experimenting with steam engines: 2_____	
Year and day of the week when he built the modern steam engine: 3_____ , 4_____	Year he sold his first steam engine: 5_____
Year he stopped working: 6_____	Year he died: 7_____

When James Watt was born in 1736 in Greenock, Scotland, simple steam engines were already used to pump water out of coal mines. These pumps weren't invented by Watt, of course, and nobody knows who first made them. However, Watt is usually called the inventor of the 'modern' steam engine.

The story begins with young Watt, sitting by the fireplace in the little cottage he grew up in. He loved watching the steam rising from his parents' boiling tea kettle in their cottage, and this was the beginning of a lifelong fascination with steam.

In 1763, somebody brought him a model of Thomas Newcomen's steam-pumping engine that was broken and didn't work any more. He asked Watt if he could try and repair the machine.

Watt was excited, and it didn't take him long to get the model going. He was fascinated by it, but soon noticed that it wasted a lot of energy because the cylinder was used both for heating and for cooling. For weeks, he carried out lots of experiments.

On a Sunday afternoon in 1765, while the inventor was going for a walk, he had an idea. He thought that he could make the steam engine much more powerful if he made a second container where the cooling could take place and the steam could be condensed, while the cylinder was kept at the same temperature all the time.

The next morning, he built a prototype and was very happy when he saw that it worked. Watt had invented a much more efficient steam engine.

Shortly afterwards, James Watt and Matthew Boulton started a business together and began selling the Watt steam engine in 1775. Watt's engines were used in the coal mines, but they were much better than the ones used when he was a boy. His engines were also used for transportation and in the textile industry.

Watt was very successful as a businessman, and when he retired in 1800, he'd become a wealthy man. He died in August 1819.

CONSOLIDATION

LISTENING

1 🔊 **32 Listen to the conversation. Tick (✓) A, B or C.**

1 What is the weather like as they are talking?

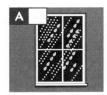 A 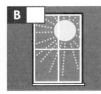 B 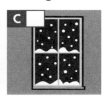 C

2 The boy says that spring is already starting. How does he know?

 A  B  C

3 Where does the girl think they could have a party?

 A  B 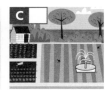 C

2 🔊 **32 Listen again. Mark the sentences T (true) or F (false).**

0 It's summer. | F |
1 The boy would like to stop winter happening. | |
2 The boy likes to hear birds singing. | |
3 The boy thinks they could have a party at the end of the month. | |
4 You can get twenty people into the flat. | |
5 The girl's parents have a big garden. | |

GRAMMAR

3 Complete the sentences. Use one word.

0 I go running every morning, and so ___*does*___ my friend Monica.

1 I wish you _____ here – but you aren't!

2 When I was younger, I _____ to think there were monsters under my bed!

3 A I really don't like cold showers.

  B _____ do I!

4 You can't come? That's a shame. I really wish you _____ .

4 Correct the sentences.

0 My sister doesn't like science, and so do I.
  My sister doesn't like science, and neither do I.

1 If I knew the answer, I told you.

_____

2 He's read this book, isn't he?

_____

3 I wish my sister is nicer to me.

_____

4 I wish I can go out tonight, but I've got homework.

_____

VOCABULARY

5 Complete the crossword.

Down

0 I think we're going to move later … year.
3 I saw this big dog. It was running … me. I was so scared.
4 I'll come and see you the … after tomorrow.
6 He's a little late, but he'll be here … too long.
8 We're going to … a DJ for the party.

Across

1 It's a … party – it's all about sport.
2 Who … the telephone?
5 I was scared of the dog so I ran … from it.
7 She's a scientist – she does … into new materials for building.
9 Our party is on the 18th, two weeks from … .
10 I'm writing a … list for the party – I'm inviting lots of people!

DIALOGUE

6 Complete the conversation. Use the phrases in the list.

~~forgotten about~~ | In other words, | That's a shame
round and round | thank goodness | lucky you
What do you reckon | there's nothing wrong with

HAYLEY Hi, Max. Listen, I want to say sorry for yesterday. I didn't mean to get angry. I'm sorry I said those things.

MAX Oh, that's OK, Hayley. I've
⁰ _forgotten about_ it already.

HAYLEY Really? ¹_____, you're OK with it?

MAX Sure. I think we should still be friends. ²_____?

HAYLEY I think that's brilliant. Thanks! And I promise I won't speak to you like that again.

MAX Well, you know, ³_____ getting angry. I mean, it happens to everyone. But sometimes people say things they don't really mean.

HAYLEY Yes, you're right of course. And honestly, I don't get angry like that very often – ⁴_____!

MAX Well, ⁵_____! I wish I could say the same.

HAYLEY Oh? Do you often get angry?

MAX Yeah, I get angry a lot, and I get bad thoughts that go ⁶_____ inside my head. Oh, anyway, let's not talk about that. Let's go get some coffee.

HAYLEY I'm sorry, I can't. I've got to go home.

MAX ⁷_____. But OK, another day. See you tomorrow, Hayley.

READING

7 Read the article. Match the missing sentences with the spaces A–E.

0 and meet to speak it   ☐ D
1 when *Star Trek* included them   ☐
2 in the 1960s and 1970s   ☐
3 the deepest parts of outer space   ☐
4 played by William Shatner   ☐

One of the greatest successes ever in science fiction is the TV series *Star Trek*. The person who got the idea for the story was Gene Roddenberry, and the very first episode went on air in 1966. The series features a spaceship – the Starship Enterprise – that has gone out into space on a mission to explore **[A]** and to make contact with other civilisations. At the time, it was probably the best science fiction on TV or in the movies, and the series was remarkable because members of the crew of the Enterprise included women and people of different races, something that TV **[B]** didn't show very often.

Some years after the original series finished, a new series called *Star Trek: The Next Generation* was created, with Patrick Stewart as Jean-Luc Picard, the captain of the Enterprise – a quite different figure from the original Captain Kirk, **[C]**.

Star Trek is about 50 years old, but it still has an incredible cult following. There are 'Trekkie' conventions in many places every year. Among the Enterprise's enemies were the Klingons, from the planet Klingon, and a whole Klingon language has been developed. People learn it **[D]**. There are references to the show in many books, plays and TV programmes. In *The Big Bang Theory*, for example, some of the characters know every episode by heart.

And it's also interesting to observe that some things that were fiction **[E]** are not fiction any more. Mobile phones and sliding doors, for example, seemed incredible in the early episodes, but now they are part of our everyday lives.

WRITING

8 Write a short text (about 120–150 words) about a science fiction book, film or TV programme that you really like or really dislike. Include the following information:

- what the book / film / TV programme is called
- what it is about
- what you like / dislike about it

9 WHAT A JOB!

GRAMMAR

The passive: present simple and past simple SB p.86

1 ★☆☆ **Mark the sentences A (present active), B (present passive), C (past active) or D (past passive).**

0 Our house wasn't built very well. `D`

1 The rubbish bins are emptied every Monday. ☐

2 We were late for school again yesterday. ☐

3 They're Polish. ☐

4 Dad wasn't in a good mood this morning. ☐

5 The weather's horrible outside. ☐

6 We were beaten in the final by Tom and Ed. ☐

7 She's protected by three men at all times. ☐

2 ★★☆ **Complete the conversation with the words in the list.**

~~were asked~~ | wasn't asked | aren't called
were you asked | ask | asked | was asked | are called
was offered | offered | were called | was called

OLLIE How was the job interview, Anita?

ANITA It was OK. There were ten of us. We
⁰ _were asked_ to wait and then we
¹ _____ into the interview room one by one.

OLLIE What kind of questions ² _____?

ANITA First I ³ _____ the usual kind, but then they ⁴ _____ really strange ones.

OLLIE Like what?

ANITA OK, here's one: 'You ⁵ _____ Tom. How is your life different?'

OLLIE But you ⁶ _____ Tom. You're a girl!

ANITA I guess it's a way to see how imaginative I am.

OLLIE Did they ⁷ _____ you why you want the job?

ANITA No, I ⁸ _____ that one.

OLLIE Oh. So what happened after the interview?

ANITA Well, after an hour I ⁹ _____ back into the room. And I ¹⁰ _____ the job!

OLLIE What?!

ANITA They ¹¹ _____ me the job. I got it!

3 ★★★ **Complete the second sentence so that it means the same as the first. Use no more than three words.**

0 Someone found my wallet outside the school.
My _wallet was found_ outside the school.

1 They make cars in that factory.
Cars _____ in that factory.

2 They don't charge you to use the computers.
You _____ charged to use the computers.

3 Nobody saw them leave.
They _____ when they left.

4 People lose lots of umbrellas on London buses.
Lots of umbrellas _____ on London buses.

5 An American bought the painting.
The painting _____ an American.

6 They don't cook the meals at the school.
The meals _____ at the school.

7 A famous architect designed the houses.
The houses _____ a famous architect.

4 ★★★ **Complete the text with the correct active or passive form of the verbs.**

Did you know that yesterday, more than 80 million letters and parcels ⁰ _were delivered_ (deliver) in the UK? But how does a letter get from A to B?
Of course, first it ¹ _____ (write) and ² _____ (put) in an envelope. Then stamps ³ _____ (put) on it and it ⁴ _____ (post) in a post box. A post office worker ⁵ _____ (collect) it and ⁶ _____ (take) it to a sorting office. Here, the letters ⁷ _____ (sort) by their postcodes. This ⁸ _____ (do) by a machine, but in the past it ⁹ _____ (not do) by machine – it ¹⁰ _____ (do) by hand. Then the letters ¹¹ _____ (take) by road, rail and air to their destination, where post office workers ¹² _____ (give) the letters for their round.

The passive: present continuous and present perfect `SB p.89`

5 ★☆☆ **Complete the sentences with *been* or *being*.**

0 The new supermarket is *being* opened.

1 The dog is _____ chased.

2 The paintings have _____ stolen.

3 The dog has _____ fed.

4 The criminals are _____ arrested.

5 The trees are _____ cut down.

6 The door has _____ painted.

7 The windows have _____ broken.

6 (Circle) the the correct words.

0 You can't buy her new book because it *isn't being* / (*hasn't been*) published yet.

1 The new library isn't finished – it *is still being* / *has still been* built.

2 This food is horrible – it *isn't being* / *hasn't been* cooked properly.

3 The food isn't ready yet – it's *being* / *been* cooked.

4 Look at this red spot on my arm. *I'm being* / *I've been* bitten by a mosquito.

5 He's in an ambulance now. He's *being* / *been* taken to hospital.

6 There's no cake left – it's all *being* / *been* eaten!

7 I haven't got my computer right now – it's *being* / *been* fixed.

7 ★★★ **Rewrite the active sentences in the passive form and the passive sentences in the active form.**

0 Someone has shot the president.
The president *has been shot.*

1 The police are questioning him.
He _____

2 The dog is being given a bath by Wendy.
Wendy _____

3 A new café has been opened near my house.
They _____

4 They've just made a new *Star Wars* film.
A new *Star Wars* film _____

5 A professional chef is cooking the meal.
The meal _____

6 The house is being rented by students.
Students _____

7 They've eaten all the food.
All the food _____

8 ★★ **Complete the email with the present perfect passive or present continuous passive form of the verbs.**

Dear Mum,

Our new house is going well and the money [0] *hasn't run out* (not run out) yet! I'm sending you a photo. As you can see, a lot [1]_____ (do) since you were here in September. The walls [2]_____ (build) and the roof [3]_____ (put on). The doors and the windows [4]_____ (not put) on yet – next week, hopefully. At the moment, most of the work [5]_____ (do) inside the house. As I'm writing, the walls [6]_____ (paint) and the kitchen [7]_____ (fit). The bathroom [8]_____ already _____ (fit). Three more weeks and it will all be over. You must come and see it.

Love, Phil

GET IT RIGHT!

Present simple passive vs. present perfect passive

Learners often use the present simple passive where the present perfect passive is required.

✓ *I have been given a new phone for my birthday.*
✗ ~~*I am given a new phone for my birthday.*~~

Complete the sentences with the correct form of the verbs in brackets.

0 I am sorry to inform you that the concert *has been cancelled* (cancel).

1 We've been raising money for charity and so far we _____ (give) £150!

2 All the best smartphones _____ (make) in Asia.

3 Nowadays, this type of shark _____ (find) only in North America.

4 I need help – my computer _____ (attack) by a virus.

5 My bike _____ (steal)! How am I going to get home?.

6 In England potato chips _____ (call) crisps.

VOCABULARY

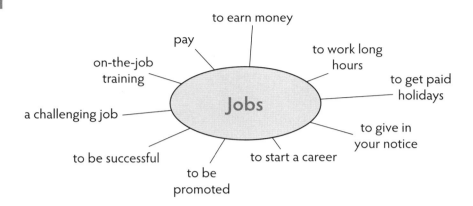

to earn money
pay
on-the-job training
to work long hours
a challenging job
to get paid holidays
to be successful
to give in your notice
to be promoted
to start a career

Jobs

work as / in / for
She works **as** a teacher.
She works **in** television.
She works **for** a big bank.

work vs. job
She's got **a** good **job**.
It's difficult **work**, but I like it.

Time expressions with *in*

in the end
in two weeks' time
in the next few years
in the past
in summer
in June
in three hours
in a day

Key words in context

candle	There was no electricity, so we had to use **candles** for light.
cameraman	He's a **cameraman**. He's filmed all over the world.
charity	She gave all her money to a **charity** that looks after children with no parents.
disability	The Paralympics are for athletes with **disabilities**.
disabled	She can't walk, but she doesn't think of herself as being **disabled**.
frame	That's a lovely photo of you. You should put it in a **frame**.
metal	It's made of **metal**. That's why it's so heavy.
operate	Do you know how to **operate** this camera? I can't get it to work.
pole	If you use this **pole**, I'm sure you can knock the ball out of the tree.
sponsor	I want to raise money for the hospital. I'm going to swim five miles and I want people to **sponsor** me.
wheelchair	She broke both legs and was in a **wheelchair** for six months.

Jobs `SB p.86`

1 ★★☆ **Complete the text with the words in the list.**

~~long~~ | on-the-job | paid | promoted | successful
earn | challenging | career | pay | notice

My job is the worst job in the world. I work really
⁰ _long_ hours – 8 am to 8 pm every day. The
¹_____ is terrible and I only just ²_____
enough money to live on. I don't get ³_____
holidays and I lose money if I need to take time off.
When I started, they promised me ⁴_____
training. Well, they showed me how to make a cup of
tea and that was it! I've been here ten years and I still
haven't been ⁵_____ . I'm doing the same job I did
when I started. And it isn't really the most ⁶_____
job. I mean, I think I could probably do it in my sleep.
On my first day here I was so excited. I really thought
this was the start of my ⁷_____ . I thought I'd soon
be a ⁸_____ businessman earning loads of money.
Well, I was wrong.
I know what you're thinking. Why don't I give in my
⁹_____ ? I can't – the boss is my dad!

work as / in / for `SB p.89`

2 ★★☆ **Complete the sentences with the words in the list.**

~~travel agent~~ | IT | tourism | modelling agency
online gaming company | model
software engineer | fashion | travel company

She works as a ⁰ _travel agent_ .
She works in ¹_____ .
She works for a small ²_____ .

He works for an ³_____ .
He works as a ⁴_____ .
He works in ⁵_____ .

He works in ⁶_____ .
He works as a ⁷_____ .
He works for a ⁸_____ .

3 ★★☆ **Write about a person you know.**

1 My _____ works as _____ .
2 He/She works in _____ .
3 He/She works for _____ .

work vs. job `SB p.89`

4 ★☆☆ (Circle) **the correct words.**

0 I've got a brilliant (job) / work. I love it.
1 I had a lot of job / work to do and I didn't get to bed until 1 am.
2 A lot of people lost their jobs / works when they closed the shop.
3 She starts her new job / work next week.
4 I like what I do, but it's very hard job / work at times.
5 We need to create more jobs / works in this country.
6 The teacher was really happy with my job / work.
7 Do you take job / work home with you sometimes?

WordWise `SB p.91`
Time expressions with *in*

5 ★★☆ **Match the sentence halves.**

0	What did you decide to do	f
1	We hope to get married	
2	People did things differently	
3	How many hot dogs can you eat	
4	He ran the 100 metres	
5	The World Cup is usually	
6	We often go skiing	
7	I can't believe the school holidays start	

a in the past.
b in two weeks' time.
c in the next few years.
d in the winter.
e in under 10 seconds.
f in the end?
g in June and July.
h in five minutes?

6 ★★★ **Write a sentence about each of these things.**

1 Something you did in the past (but you don't do now).
2 Something you're going to do in 10 minutes' time.
3 Something you want to do in the next few years.
4 Something you always do in summer.
5 Something you can do in less than 10 seconds.
6 Something that always happens in December.

READING

1 [REMEMBER AND CHECK] Answer the questions. Then check your answers in the text on page 85 of the Student's Book.

0 Who worked for only half a year? ___Ben___

1 Who earned about £33 a day for the job? _____

2 Who doesn't earn any money? _____

3 Who works from home? _____

4 Who beat thousands of people to get the job? _____

5 Who worked for a furniture company? _____

2 Read the magazine article. How is Richard different from Erin and Nathan?

_____

Everyone gets nervous in a job interview, but we want to know about the worst interview you've ever had – or given!

I had a job interview for a big advertising company in London. At that time I lived more than 200 miles from London, but I really wanted this job, so I took a three-hour train journey and spent more than £100 on a return ticket. The train was half an hour late, so I spent another £20 to get a taxi across London to the offices of the company. I got to the reception desk just in time and was taken straight into the interview room. The interviewer invited me to sit down and asked me his first question.

'Do you speak French?'

'No, I don't,' I told him.

'Oh, I'm sorry,' he replied. 'We really need someone who speaks French.'

He stood up, shook my hand and thanked me for coming. What a waste of time and money.

ERIN

I once had a job interview with an important law firm. More than 300 people applied for the job and only ten of us were invited for an interview. The interview was exhausting. It lasted for more than an hour and I was asked lots of really difficult questions.

However, I was pleased with my answers and I was pretty sure that the interview was going well. I was right. At the end, the interviewer offered me the job and stood up to shake my hand. I stood up too, but my leg was dead from sitting down for so long. As soon as I stood up, I fell down backwards. Unfortunately, I was shaking the interviewer's hand and I forgot to let go. As I fell, I pulled him down with me onto the floor. It was very embarrassing. Amazingly, I still got the job.

NATHAN

I once interviewed a man for a job. He came into my office wearing a pair of headphones. I invited him to sit down, thinking he was going to take off the headphones, but he didn't. So I asked him, 'Would you mind taking off the headphones? It might be easier to interview you.'

'Oh, it's OK,' he replied. 'I can hear you OK and I find listening to music helps me relax.' He wasn't offered the job. Neither was the man who brought his dog into the interview room and asked me if I could get him a bowl of water for the dog to drink!

RICHARD

3 Read the article again. Mark the sentences T (true), F (false) or DS (the text doesn't say).

0 Erin spent over £100 to get to her interview. **T**

1 Erin got the money back for her train and taxi. ☐

2 Nathan wasn't confident in his interview. ☐

3 Nathan had to compete with over 300 people to get the job. ☐

4 The interviewer wasn't happy when Nathan pulled him onto the floor. ☐

5 Nathan still works at the law firm. ☐

6 The man wore headphones because he had a hearing problem. ☐

7 Richard only gave one of the men a job. ☐

4 Which of these stories do you think is the funniest? Why?

_____

_____

Instructions vs. processes

1 Read the article. Match texts A and B with the pictures.

1

2

Working world

This week we visit a professional candle factory to see how candles are made and then a candle artist tells us how to make a homemade candle.

A

First, lots of wicks are tied to a wooden frame and the wax is melted in huge pans.

Then the frame with the wicks is dipped slowly in and out of the wax.

Each time the frame is dipped, a small coat of wax sticks to the wick and the candle gets bigger.

This is done until the candles are thick enough.

After this, the candles are left to dry. Finally, when they are dry, they are cut from the frame and packed into boxes.

B

First, prepare a mould. You could use a glass jar. Place a wick into the mould and attach it to a clip that lies across the top of the mould.

Next, melt the wax. Do this by putting the wax in a pan and then putting this pan in a larger pan of boiling water. When it is melted, you can add colouring and a perfume if you want to.

Carefully pour the melted wax into the mould.

When the wax is hard, cut the top of the wick to a suitable length. If you're using a flexible mould, gently take the candle out and cut the wick at the bottom of the candle.

2 the correct words.

1 *Text A / Text B* uses a lot of examples of the passive.

2 Text A *describes a process / gives instructions*.

3 *Text A / Text B* uses the pronoun *you*.

4 Text B *describes a process / gives instructions*.

3 Plan a text that describes a process.

- Think of a process that you know well or research one on the Internet. For example, it could be how milk gets to the supermarket or how Oscars are awarded.
- Identify four or five different stages of the process and put them in chronological order.
- Ask your teacher to help with any difficult vocabulary.
- Write mini-paragraphs of a few sentences each to describe each stage of the process.
- Remember to use the passive when it's needed.
- Link your paragraphs together using staging words: *first, then, after that, next, when, finally*.

4 Write your text (100–150 words).

Writing tip: instructions vs. processes

- When we write about processes, we often use the passive voice. This is because the person who does the actions isn't important and we don't need to know who it is.
- When we give instructions, we often talk directly to our reader and use the imperative. This makes the text more personal.

LISTENING

1 🔊33 Listen to the conversations. Write the names of the speakers. There is one name that you don't need.

~~Ben~~ | Rob | Jim | Ollie | Kate | Eve | Debbie

1 _Ben_ and _____

2 _____ and _____

3 _____ and _____

2 🔊33 Listen again and answer the questions.

0 What are they all raising money for?
   To help the victims of an earthquake in China.

1 How far is the sponsored walk?
   _____

2 When and where is the book sale?
   _____

3 What's Jim going to do on Friday afternoon?
   _____

4 Why doesn't Debbie want to do the sponsored dance?
   _____

DIALOGUE

1 Put the words in order to make phrases.

0 us / join / want / do / you / to
   Do you want to join us?

1 in / me / count
   _____

2 going / there / to / you / are / be / ?
   _____

3 but / love / can't / I'd / to / I
   _____

4 you / in / are / so / ?
   _____

5 not / sorry / time / no / this
   _____

2 Choose two of the phrases from Exercise 1 and use them to write a four-line conversation.

A *Hi, Beth. Where are you going?*

B *I'm going to meet Jo in town. We're going to have lunch. Do you want to join us?*

A *I'd love to, but I can't. I've got to help my mum.*

B *Never mind. Maybe next time.*

   _____

   _____

   _____

   _____

PHRASES FOR FLUENCY

1 Put the conversation in the correct order.

☐ IAN No, I haven't. I didn't make the mess. Tim did.

☐ IAN I've got to do some research for my History project.

☐ IAN Mum! Surely you don't think I'd do that!

☐ IAN Sounds fair. Thanks, Mum.

1️⃣ IAN Mum, can I use your computer for a while?

☐ MUM No – you'd never do that. By the way, have you tidied your room yet?

☐ MUM What do you want it for?

☐ MUM That's not the point. I asked you to do it. Tidy the room and then you can use the computer.

☐ MUM OK, as long as it is for that and not for playing games!

2 Complete the conversations with the phrases in the list.

~~surely~~ | for a while | sounds | as long as
by the way | that's not the point

CONVERSATION 1

A Can you help me with my homework?

B Sorry, I'm busy.

A ⁰ _Surely_ you've got ten minutes free.

B Well, ¹_____ , anyway. It's your homework. You should do it on your own.

A OK, if that's how you feel. Oh, ²_____ , don't ask me if you can borrow my bike this weekend. Because you can't.

CONVERSATION 2

A We haven't been dancing ³_____ . Shall we go this weekend?

B ⁴_____ great. ⁵_____ we don't have to invite my sister too.

A Why not?

B I just don't want her to come.

Pronunciation

/tʃ/ and /dʒ/ consonant sounds

Go to page 120. 🔊

Help with listening: identifying individual words (1)

1 ◀♪36 **Read the conversation. See if you can write one word in each space without listening. Then listen and check.**

BOY Hey. How are you ?

GIRL Good. ⁰ _And_ you?

BOY Yes, not bad, thanks. ¹_____ I've got to go ²_____ London tomorrow. ³_____ do a test.

GIRL What sort ⁴_____ test?

BOY Oh, it's OK – not a test ⁵_____ any medical things.

GIRL So it's a test ⁶_____ what?

BOY To see if I ⁷_____ play in the England under-17 football team!

GIRL Really? Wow – fantastic! Well done! I knew you ⁸_____ good at football, ⁹_____ not ¹⁰_____ good ¹¹_____ that!

BOY Thanks. It's all day – starts ¹²_____ eight ¹³_____ finishes ¹⁴_____ five.

GIRL Right. And when ¹⁵_____ ¹⁶_____ know the result?

BOY Not sure. I'll have ¹⁷_____ wait.

GIRL Well, good luck, then. I wish I ¹⁸_____ going with you!

Tip: identifying individual words

- Something that is very important about spoken English is that very often, 'small words' aren't pronounced strongly. Speakers use something called 'weak sounds'.

- For example, the word *and* is pronounced /ən/ in these examples:

  We went with John **and** Stuart.
  I love fish **and** chips.

- It's often the same (but not always!) with these words: *an, are, as, at, but, can, do, for, of, to, was, were* and *you*.

- ◀♪36 Listen to the conversation in Exercise 1 again. Pay attention to how the missing words are pronounced.

---

2 ◀♪37 **Listen to the sentences and complete them with one word in each space.**

1 My favourite things ⁰ _to_ eat ¹_____ fish ²_____ chips ³_____ green peas.

2 The film ⁴_____ bad, ⁵_____ the dinner ⁶_____ worse!

3 I ⁷_____ come ⁸_____ eight, ⁹_____ I may be late.

4 The questions ¹⁰_____ really difficult ¹¹_____ me ¹²_____ answer.

5 Where ¹³_____ ¹⁴_____ live?

6 She ¹⁵_____ sing pretty well, ¹⁶_____ not ¹⁷_____ well ¹⁸_____ ¹⁹_____ old friend ²⁰_____ mine.

10 KEEP HEALTHY

GRAMMAR

Past perfect simple SB p.94

1 ★☆☆ **Match the pictures with the sentences.**

0 When he arrived at the platform, the train had left. `C`

1 When he arrived at the platform, the train left. ☐

2 When I saw her, she fell off her bike. ☐

3 When I saw her, she had fallen off her bike. ☐

2 ★☆☆ **Match the sentence halves.**

0 I recognised her face, `f`

1 They got to the theatre ☐

2 As soon as he closed the door, ☐

3 My notebook didn't switch on ☐

4 I didn't think I'd said anything funny, ☐

5 When the exam finished, ☐

a but he couldn't stop laughing.

b because I'd forgotten to recharge it.

c I hadn't answered all the questions.

d he knew he'd left his key inside.

e ten minutes after the play had started.

f but I couldn't remember where I'd met her.

3 ★★☆ **Complete the sentences. Use the past perfect form of the verbs in the list.**

see | tidy | do | not tidy | not do | not see | have

0 I didn't watch the film because I __'d seen__ it before.

1 Amy didn't invite Jack to the party because they _____ a fight earlier in the week.

2 Daisy's dad was angry with her because she _____ her bedroom.

3 I didn't have to take the dog for a walk because Joey _____ already _____ it.

4 The house was looking really clean because Mum and Dad _____ everything away.

5 Kim had to miss her break time because she _____ her homework.

6 The driver almost caused an accident because he _____ the red light.

4 ★★★ **Complete the text with either the past simple or the past perfect form of the verbs.**

Tina ⁰ __had eaten__ (eat) three and a half biscuits and was starting on her fourth when she ¹_____ (start) making strange noises. I² _____ (look) at her and I ³_____ (know) immediately that a large piece of her biscuit ⁴_____ (get) stuck in her throat. Then I ⁵_____ (remember) that years ago I ⁶_____ (attend) a first aid course and that they ⁷_____ (teach) us how to help someone in this situation. I ⁸_____ (run) around Tina,⁹_____ (put) my arms around her waist,¹⁰_____ (join) my hand together in front of her and ¹¹_____ (pull) as hard as I could. Then I ¹²_____ (hear) a little cry from Tina and I ¹³_____ (knew) that the food ¹⁴_____ (come) out. Tina ¹⁵_____ (give) me a big hug. That first aid lesson ¹⁶_____ (probably save) her life.

Past perfect continuous `SB p.97`

5 ★ ☆ ☆ **Put the words in order to make sentences.**

0   been / hours / talking / we / for / had
We had been talking for hours.

1   been / to / I / them / hadn't / listening
_____

2   waiting / long / you / how / had / been?
_____

3   crying / had / morning / she / been / all
_____

4   well / I / been / hadn't / very / feeling
_____

5   had / been / how / it / raining / long?
_____

Past perfect continuous vs. past perfect simple `SB p.97`

6 ★ ☆ ☆ (Circle) **the best options.**

0   I was disappointed. I *had saved I* (had been saving) all year and I still didn't have enough money.

1   Dad *had cooked / had been cooking* all morning and the kitchen smelled great.

2   They *hadn't eaten / hadn't been eating* anything all day and they were really hungry.

3   Kevin *had watched / had been watching* the film five times and he still didn't really understand it.

4   They *had walked / had been walking* 50 km before they saw anyone.

5   She failed the test because she *hadn't written / hadn't been writing* enough.

7 ★★ ☆ **Complete the text with the words in the list.**

~~had been having~~ | hadn't called | hadn't listened
had been snowing | had been waiting
hadn't been sleeping | had written

I ⁰ *had been having*   headaches for a week and
I ¹ _____ well, so my dad made an appointment for me to see the doctor. We took a taxi to the doctor's because it ² _____ all morning.

We arrived at 3 pm and sat down. We
³ _____ for an hour and they still
⁴ _____ me when Dad went to talk to the receptionist. My appointment was for 2 pm! Dad
⁵ _____ properly on the phone and
he ⁶ _____ down the wrong time!

8 ★★★ **Complete the sentences with the verbs. Use one past perfect simple form and one past perfect continuous form in each pair.**

0   (spend)
   A She didn't have any money left because she
   *had spent* it all on a new dress.
   B They *had been spending* too much money for years and now they had none left.

1   (play)
   A He _____ only _____ football for five minutes when he broke his leg.
   B They _____ all the games in the house and now they were bored.

2   (drink)
   A He _____ four glasses of water and now he really needed the toilet.
   B He _____ the cup of coffee for more than an hour and now it was cold.

3   (not look)
   A She _____ where she was going and that's why she crashed.
   B She _____ at her diary that day and that's why she missed her appointment.

GET IT RIGHT!

Past perfect continuous vs. past continuous

Learners sometimes use the past continuous when the past perfect continuous is required.

✓ We **had been training** for weeks, but we lost.
✗ We ~~were training~~ for weeks, but we lost.

Complete the sentences with the correct form of the verb in brackets.

0   I found his phone under the chair where he
   *had been sitting* (sit).

1   We met by accident when she _____ (walk) her dog.

2   When I saw him, he _____ (carry) a rucksack.

3   I _____ (wait) for hours, so I was very happy when he called.

4   I _____ (work) all day, so I decided to go out.

5   He _____ (talk) on his phone when the fire alarm went off.

VOCABULARY

Word list

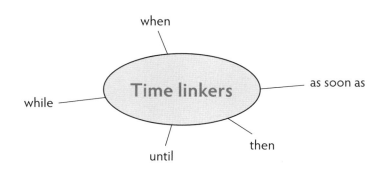

when
while — Time linkers — as soon as
until
then

Illness: collocations

take exercise

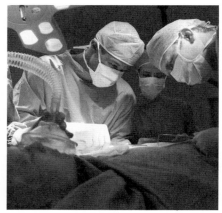

have an operation

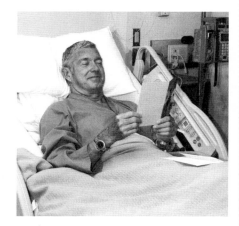

get better

make an appointment

see a doctor

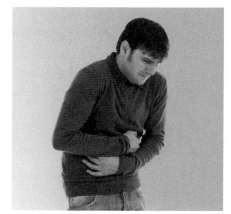

feel sick

Key words in context

annually	He has a strange job. He gets paid **annually** and has to live on that money for a year.
brave	The doctor gave him a lollipop for being really **brave** when he went to hospital.
cancer	**Cancer** is one of the biggest killers in the world.
heart attack	You shouldn't play football at your age. You'll have a **heart attack**.
infection	He cut his knee and then got a nasty **infection** in it.
lack	Many people in Africa **lack** clean water.
memory	I've got a terrible **memory**. I can never remember anything.
nearby	They live **nearby** – about ten minutes away.
overcome	He had a serious illness, but he fought hard and managed to **overcome** it.
popular	She's a really **popular** teacher. All the kids like her.
suffer	He died quickly. He didn't **suffer** a lot.

Time linkers SB p.94

1 ★☆☆ **Complete the sentences with the words in the list.**

~~when~~ | then | while | as soon as | until

0   _When_ I'm 17, I'm going to go to university.

1   _____ I'm old enough, I'm going to learn to drive.

2   I'm going to meet the right girl and _____ I'm going to get married.

3   I'm not going to have children _____ I'm 30.

4   I'm going to work in a restaurant _____ I'm at university.

2 ★★★ **Complete the sentences so they are true for you.**

0   When I'm 18, I'm going to _get a job._

1   As soon as I have enough money, I'm going to

   _____

2   I'm going to finish school and then _____

   _____

3   I'll probably live with my parents until _____

   _____

4   I'm going to _____ while I _____

   _____

Illness: collocations SB p.97

3 ★★☆ **Find five more verbs and five nouns or adjectives to make illness collocations.**

H	A	V	E	A	S	B	D	D	I	N
P	O	H	I	J	V	I	O	W	E	O
Q	A	E	U	B	M	E	C	X	Y	I
D	B	X	I	M	M	W	T	K	S	T
T	N	E	M	T	N	I	O	P	P	A
A	S	R	T	X	C	S	R	B	F	R
K	G	C	L	T	K	T	H	L	F	E
E	J	I	H	J	E	G	S	E	E	P
C	F	S	L	G	L	R	C	R	E	O
K	L	E	K	A	M	J	C	H	L	R

0   _FEEL SICK_ _____

1   _____

2   _____

3   _____

4   _____

5   _____

4 ★★☆ **Put the letters in order to make collocations.**

0   leef ciks   _feel sick_

1   ese a rctood   _____

2   amek na mpitntpoean _____

3   vaeh na oiranpteo _____

4   teg teertb   _____

5   etka rome scexiere _____

5 ★★☆ **Complete the text with collocations from Exercise 4. Use the correct form of the verbs.**

I was [0] _feeling sick_ one day a few months ago. I didn't think much about it, but the next day I was still feeling ill and I was also feeling very tired. It was the same the next day and the day after that. My wife told me I should [1]_____. Now, I don't really like going to the doctor's, but I was starting to get a bit worried. Something just didn't feel right. So I phoned the surgery that afternoon to [2]_____ for the next day.

The doctor did a few tests and he seemed really quite worried. In fact, he was so worried that he phoned immediately for an ambulance. I was rushed to hospital, where they did more tests. Finally, after about five hours, a doctor came and saw me. He said I could have a heart attack at any moment and that I needed to [3]_____ immediately.

It was a real shock, but what could I say? So I followed the doctor's orders and spent the next few months [4]_____. I went for a check-up the other day and the doctor says I'm fine. I just need to eat a little less and [5]_____.

6 ★★★ **Complete the conversations.**

1   A My dad's got to h _ave_ an o _peration_ on Monday.

    B Oh. I hope it goes well and he g_____ b_____ soon.

2   A Did you s_____ the d_____ yesterday?

    B Yes, I did. He told me to t_____ more e_____ .

3   A I'm f_____ really s_____ .

    B You'd better m_____ an a_____ with the doctor.

READING

1 **REMEMBER AND CHECK** Put the events from Phoebe Snetsinger's life in order. Then check your answers in the article on page 93 of the Student's Book.

She sees a Rufous-necked Wood Rail. ☐

Her book is published. ☐

She becomes interested in birds. ☐ 1

She is in a fatal accident. ☐

She is given a year to live. ☐

Her disease returns. ☐

She sets a new world record. ☐

She takes her total to over 8,400 species. ☐

Belle the spider-dog

When Belle was only a few months old, she was left at a home for unwanted dogs. It was immediately clear that she had a serious problem. Her legs were completely bent out of shape. They looked like the legs of a spider. Belle had great difficulty walking or moving about and preferred to lie in the corner and watch as all the other dogs of her age played around her.

The owner of the home felt really sorry for the poor dog. Belle was a really sweet loveable dog, but it was obvious how serious the problem was. Belle needed medical attention urgently and the owner was afraid that the vet might suggest that the dog should be put to sleep.

She called a vet in to take a look at Belle. The vet carefully examined the dog. The good news was that he could do an operation on the legs. The bad news was that it was an expensive operation costing around £3,000. The owner of the home knew she didn't have the money to help. The vet also had some very annoying information. This operation was very easy on a young puppy a few days old, but at Belle's age it was a lot more difficult.

Then the owner had an idea. She posted photos of Belle and her legs online, along with her story, and asked for money to help with the costs of the operation. The response was incredible and they soon had the money for the vet. Belle went through two operations, which involved breaking her legs and resetting them. Now, after several weeks of getting better, Belle has recovered and can jump around and play with all the other dogs. She will need special care and attention for the rest of her life, but at least she won't need any more operations.

Thanks to the kindness of dog lovers all over the country and the talents of a vet, Belle is enjoying the kind of exercise that all dogs love.

2 **Read the article quickly and answer the questions.**

1 How many operations did Belle have?

_____

_____

2 How many operations does she still need?

_____

3 **Read the text again. Mark the sentences T (true), F (false) or DS (the text doesn't say).**

0 Belle's legs were bent because of a problem at birth. ☐ DS

1 Belle walked like a spider. ☐

2 Belle has a good personality. ☐

3 The owner called a vet in to put Belle down. ☐

4 Belle's problem had become very expensive. ☐

5 People online didn't really care about Belle's situation. ☐

6 Belle isn't a very sociable dog. ☐

7 Belle still lives at the dogs' home. ☐

DEVELOPING WRITING

Stories

1   **Read the first part of the story and find two mistakes in the picture.**

POSTED: TODAY

I knew something was wrong when I felt the pain. It was a wet and windy day. It was raining hard. I'd been playing football with some friends in our local park. They were still playing, but I was sitting on the floor, holding my ankle in pain. I looked down at it. It was already twice as big as usual and it was turning purple. I'd been running towards the goal when someone had kicked me from behind. I'd fallen down badly and not moved since.

One boy told me to get up. Nobody else seemed to notice me. They carried on playing around me. After about another ten minutes, they decided to stop playing and they all walked off the pitch. I couldn't believe it. I called out and finally two of them came back to talk to me. When I showed them my ankle, they were shocked. They helped carry me to a café in the park and they called an ambulance. I was taken to hospital. As soon as the doctor saw my leg, he knew it was broken. I needed a small operation. While I was in hospital, my friends all came to visit me and say sorry. They also bought me a huge box of chocolates. I have forgiven them.

Writing tip: finding ideas

One of the most difficult parts of writing a story can be coming up with a good idea. However, don't worry too much if an idea doesn't come immediately. A simple idea, well written, is all that's needed. A lot of good stories follow the very basic pattern of setting up a problem and then showing how it gets solved (or not). Try and use this pattern to help you.

When you're given a first line, you need to use it to start your story. You should also use it to get ideas. Ask yourself questions like 'why?', 'who?' and 'what happened next?'. The answers can help you plan your narrative.

Think carefully about how you use past tenses. It's always good to try and use a selection of these.

Remember:
- Use the past simple for most of the main action.
- Use the past continuous to set up a background to the events and create an atmosphere.
- Also use the past continuous when one action interrupts another.
- Use the past perfect tenses for 'flashbacks' to take the reader back to events that happened earlier on.
- Don't forget to use time linkers like *when*, *as soon as*, *then*, *until* and *while* to help your story flow.
- Remember also to use good descriptive language, especially adjectives and adverbs, to bring your story 'alive'.

2   **Choose one of the opening lines and write a story (about 150 words).**
- I looked at the clock. I was ten minutes late for my appointment.
- I woke up after the operation and looked in the mirror.

LISTENING

1 🔊**38** Listen to the conversations and (circle) the correct option: A, B or C.

1 What exercise is Paul going to start doing?

   A running   **B** cycling   **C** swimming

2 What time is Chloë going to leave for her appointment?

   A 4.30   **B** 4.00   **C** 3.00

3 How is Lucy going to get to the football match?

   A by car   **B** by bus   **C** on foot

4 What is Julia going to wear?

   A hat and gloves   **B** coat   **C** coat, hat and gloves

DIALOGUE

1 Put the conversations in the correct order.

1

	PAUL	Yes, but I don't really like water.
	PAUL	I can't. My knees aren't very strong.
	PAUL	That's right, so I think it's going to be cycling.
1	PAUL	My doctor says I need to do some more exercise.
	SALLY	What about swimming? That's really good for the whole body.
	SALLY	Oh. So you need do something that's easier on your legs?
	SALLY	Really? Why don't you take up running?

2

	CHLOE	Of course. Just make sure you're here by about three.
	CHLOE	It's at 4.30.
	CHLOE	No, I'm leaving before that because I want to do some shopping.
	MARTIN	So you need to leave the house at about four?
1	MARTIN	What time's your doctor's appointment tomorrow?
	MARTIN	Can I get a lift with you?

3

	JIM	I'm going to take the bus. I'll see you there.
1	JIM	Are you going to the match tomorrow?
	JIM	The car? Are you mad? There'll be nowhere to park.
	LUCY	Yes, I thought I'd take the car.
	LUCY	So I'll walk then. It's always good to take a bit of exercise.

Pronunciation

/tʃ/ and /ʃ/ consonant sounds

Go to page 121. 🔊

▰▰ TRAIN TO THiNK ▰▰

Drawing conclusions

1 Read the statements and tick (✓) the correct conclusion.

0 I like all fruits.

   Apples are a fruit.

   So …

   I like apples.   ✓

   Apples are my favourite fruit.   ☐

1 Maths is the most popular subject at school.

   I'm in a Maths lesson.

   So …

   I'm doing my favourite lesson.   ☐

   Most people in my classroom are doing their favourite lesson.   ☐

2 I only wear glasses to read.

   I'm wearing my glasses.

   So …

   I'm reading a book.   ☐

   My eyes are tired.   ☐

3 I need to go to bed at 8 pm.

   It's 10 pm and we're still out.

   So …

   I've forgotten what time it is.   ☐

   I'm tired.   ☐

2 Write conclusions for these statements.

1 I always dance when I hear music.

   I'm listening to a song on the radio.

   So _____

   _____

2 Bob says yes to everything.

   I asked Bob if he wants a sandwich.

   So _____

   _____

3 His third book was his best.

   His first book was better than his second book.

   So _____

   _____

4 My birthday is one day after Bernie's.

   Yesterday was Bernie's birthday.

   So _____

Reading part 4

1 Read the text. (Circle) the correct option: A, B, C or D.

1 What is Dan's reason for writing the text?

   A to encourage young people to take up a sport

   B to show how you're never too old to start a new sport

   C to talk about how his running has changed over the years

   D to explain his love of the sport

2 How does Dan compare his running these days with when he first started?

   A He's slower and his body suffers more, but he still enjoys it as much.

   B He finds it more difficult to train.

   C He's only about ten minutes slower.

   D He isn't enjoying it as much.

3 What does he enjoy most about the half marathon races?

   A trying to go quicker each time he races

   B being cheered on by people

   C meeting up with old friends

   D beating younger people

4 Why does Dan visit schools?

   A to race the children

   B to pick up his grandchildren

   C to encourage children to do sport

   D to show that old people can still do things

5 What might Dan write in his autobiography?

   A 'In my later years, running became a really important part of my life. It kept my body and mind younger and helped me fight against getting older.'

   B 'When I was younger, I was a really competitive runner, but as I got older, I was just happy to run and I didn't really care how fast I went.'

   C 'I've always loved running. I've loved the way it's kept me healthy and I've loved the way it's brought me into contact with so many people.'

   D 'As I got older, running became more difficult. I thought about giving it up, but my doctor told me to keep going. I'm happy he did and these days I love inspiring young people to start running.'

Exam guide: multiple-choice questions

- In this question you will read a text that focuses more on someone's opinion than on facts and figures. To choose the right answer you need to understand the writer's attitudes, opinions and reason for writing the text. The first question usually focuses on the reasons why the writer has written the text and the final question usually looks at the meaning of the text as a whole. The other three questions usually pick up on information in the order that it is given in the passage.

- Read through the text quickly to understand what it is about. After this reading, think about why you feel the writer wrote this text.

- Read the text for a second time. This time, read it a lot more carefully. It's often a good idea to look at questions 1 and 5 first since they need an understanding of the whole passage.

- For questions 2, 3 and 4, find and concentrate on the parts of the text that each question is asking about and study them carefully. Remember: these questions might be asking you about the writer's opinions and not just about facts.

Dan Collins: Half marathon enthusiast

I started running half marathons in the 1960s. I'm 78 now, I've been doing them for nearly fifty years and I still get the same excitement at the beginning of each race as I always have. I don't do as many as I did. I used to run around 30 every year and in my thirties I got quite good at them. I think my personal best was around 1 hour 17 minutes, which was only ten minutes over the world record back then. These days I do about ten a year and my time is quite a bit slower. At my age you need a lot more preparation and your body doesn't recover as quickly, but it's well worth all the extra work.

There are two main reasons why I still run half marathons. Firstly, it means I'm keeping myself fit. My doctor told me that I'm healthier than most 50-year-olds. But I think the real reason why I love the sport so much is the other people it brings you into contact with. You meet other athletes and I've made many good friends over the years, but the most amazing thing is all the people who line up along the sides of the streets to cheer you on. I get more and more support the older I get.

I also spend quite a lot of time visiting schools to get children interested in doing sport. I think it's really important to get involved at an early age. It makes it so much easier to keep doing it the older you get. The kids are always really enthusiastic and they ask me loads of questions. Many of them can't believe that I'm the same age as their grandfathers. Sometimes I challenge them to a five-kilometre race. There aren't many of them that can beat me!

CONSOLIDATION

LISTENING

1 ◀)) 42 **Listen to the conversation. Tick (✓) A, B or C.**

1 What has Tracy's mother had problems with?
   A her elbow ☐
   B her wrist ☐
   C her shoulder ☐

2 Tracy's mother has the problem because of …
   A computers and tennis. ☐
   B tennis and the guitar. ☐
   C a new job indoors. ☐

3 What does Tracy's mother want to do?
   A be a waitress in a restaurant ☐
   B teach people how to cook ☐
   C learn how to cook ☐

2 ◀)) 42 **Listen again. Mark the sentences T (true) or F (false).**

0 Tracy knows that her mother's operation was successful. ☐F☐

1 Tracy's mother is not a good typist. ☐

2 Tracy's mother still plays in tennis competitions. ☐

3 Tracy's mother has told her employers that she's going to leave. ☐

4 Andy thinks that being a cook is quite easy. ☐

5 Tracy's mother will not earn as much money in her new job. ☐

VOCABULARY

3 Match the sentence halves.

0 I think you should make ☐c☐
1 I'm sure you'll feel better if you take ☐
2 The test was easy. I finished it in ☐
3 I kept working at the problem ☐
4 I left the exam room as soon as ☐
5 It was a difficult question, but in ☐
6 You're sick? Oh, I really hope you get ☐

a until I got the right answer.
b I'd finished the test.
c an appointment to see a doctor.
d the end I got the answer.
e better soon.
f some exercise.
g under an hour.

4 Complete the words.

0 The work's hard but the p _ay_____ is really good, so I don't mind.

1 She works very hard but she doesn't e_____ a lot, so it's difficult for her.

2 He did really well in the job and after three months he was p_____ .

3 I love travel, so I want to have a c_____ as a travel agent.

4 I didn't enjoy the work very much, so after a year I gave in my n_____ .

5 She left the job because the work wasn't c_____ enough for her.

GRAMMAR

5 Rewrite the sentences. Use the words in brackets.

0 They don't pay us a lot. (aren't)
   We aren't paid a lot.

1 They built a new school. (was)
   _____

2 They have promoted my sister. (been)
   _____

3 They are making another film about the *Titanic*. (made)
   _____

4 They show football on TV every day! (shown)
   _____

5 They have knocked down that building. (been)
   _____

6 Complete the text. Use the past simple, past perfect simple or past perfect continuous of the verbs.

One day my uncle [0] _left_ (leave) work very late – about 7.30 pm. He [1]_____ (be) very tired because he [2]_____ (spend) the whole afternoon writing emails. When he left, he [3]_____ (write) emails for more than three hours! He [4]_____ (start) to drive home but he got stuck in a lot of traffic because there [5]_____ (be) a very bad accident at seven o'clock. When he finally [6]_____ (get) home, it was 9.40 – he [7]_____ (drive) for almost two hours. Then he [8]_____ (realise) that he couldn't get into his house because he [9]_____ (leave) his keys on his desk in the office!

DIALOGUE

7 **Complete the conversation. Use the phrases in the list.**

~~Sounds great~~ | as long as | as soon as
have an operation | in a few weeks' time
By the way | for a while | hadn't been

JAKE	So, how was your weekend?
MARTHA	Really nice, thanks. On Sunday I went for a picnic with my family.
JAKE	⁰ *Sounds great* . I love picnics. ¹_____, how is your little brother? Someone told me that he ²_____ very well.
MARTHA	Well, that's right. He was pretty ill ³_____. The doctor said that he might need to ⁴_____. But that didn't happen, I'm happy to say. And he's OK now, thanks. He has to go back to the doctor ⁵_____, but ⁶_____ he looks after himself, things should be OK.
JAKE	Has he gone back to school yet?
MARTHA	Not yet. But he'll go back ⁷_____ he feels well enough, maybe next week. He really misses it.
JAKE	Really? Wow, I'd love a few weeks off school!

READING

8 **Read the article. Write the paragraph titles in the correct places. There are two titles you don't need.**

~~Get close to nature~~ | Surf the Internet
Think about food | Go running
Walk to work | Watch how you sit
Keep moving | Use your work area as a gym

WRITING

9 **Write a paragraph (about 120 words) about how you can keep healthy at school. Use the ideas to help you:**

- getting to school
- food
- exercise
- the way you sit / stand / walk

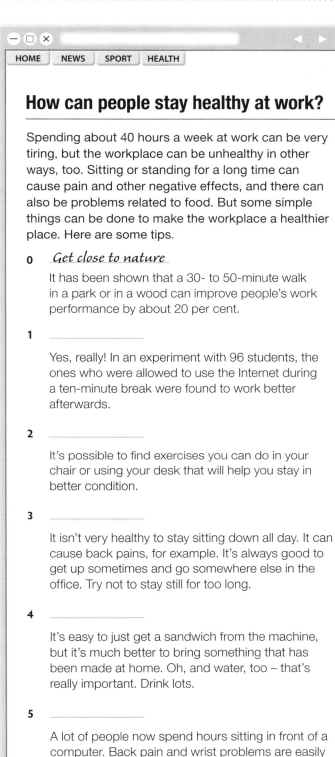

HOME | NEWS | SPORT | HEALTH

How can people stay healthy at work?

Spending about 40 hours a week at work can be very tiring, but the workplace can be unhealthy in other ways, too. Sitting or standing for a long time can cause pain and other negative effects, and there can also be problems related to food. But some simple things can be done to make the workplace a healthier place. Here are some tips.

0 *Get close to nature*

It has been shown that a 30- to 50-minute walk in a park or in a wood can improve people's work performance by about 20 per cent.

1 _____

Yes, really! In an experiment with 96 students, the ones who were allowed to use the Internet during a ten-minute break were found to work better afterwards.

2 _____

It's possible to find exercises you can do in your chair or using your desk that will help you stay in better condition.

3 _____

It isn't very healthy to stay sitting down all day. It can cause back pains, for example. It's always good to get up sometimes and go somewhere else in the office. Try not to stay still for too long.

4 _____

It's easy to just get a sandwich from the machine, but it's much better to bring something that has been made at home. Oh, and water, too – that's really important. Drink lots.

5 _____

A lot of people now spend hours sitting in front of a computer. Back pain and wrist problems are easily caused that way. It's important to pay attention to your posture (for example, the position of your back and shoulders) when you're sitting down. Keep any screen at eye level while you're working so that you don't have to put your head down to look at it!

GRAMMAR

Reported statements SB p.104

1 ★☆☆ **Put the words in order to make sentences.**

0 that / said / She / only / it / joke / was / a
She said that it was only a joke.

1 could / me / me / He / help / he / told / that
_____

2 they / said / lunch / join / would / They / for / us
_____

3 late / I / that / be / was / I / going / you / told / to
_____

4 said / before / article / the / The / had / accident / day / the / happened
_____

5 she / teacher / Our / had / told / lost / us / homework / our
_____

2 ★★★ **Write reported statements.**

0 Terry: 'I'm going to buy a car.'
Terry said *he was going to buy a car.*

1 Emily to me: 'I want to go to the concert.'
Emily told _____

2 Lucy: 'I wasn't happy with the test.'
Lucy said _____

3 Zoe to Mike: 'I haven't seen that film yet.'
Zoe told _____

4 Nigel: 'We'll be late unless we leave soon.'
Nigel said _____

5 Scarlett to Dan: 'I didn't really enjoy the party.'
Scarlett told _____

6 Jack: 'I'm not feeling very well.'
Jack said _____

7 Bella to Jo: 'I don't want to invite Tim to my party.'
Bella told _____

3 ★★★ **Read the email. Then complete the conversation.**

Hi Sofia,

Just a quick message to say that Seville is great! We got here three days ago, and we're staying in a hotel not far from the famous Real Alcázar, a group of very attractive palaces with a famous gallery. We visited it on the first day, and I was very impressed by it. We've seen a lot of fascinating sights so far – I liked the Giralda Tower most. Now we're going to spend time in the Plaza de España. I am so looking forward to this. I've heard it's one of the most beautiful squares in Spain, with a canal and bridges that look like the ones in Venice!

Tomorrow we're going to Cáceres. Mum's a bit worried because we'll be in the car for more than four hours. But Dad says it's a fascinating city – it was built by the Romans more than two thousand years ago! That's it from me. Next week we're off to France!

Hope you're OK.

Love, Lucy

SOFIA I got an email from Lucy last week. She's on holiday with her parents in Seville in Spain. She said they ⁰ _____*had*_____ got there two days before, and they ¹_____ in a hotel near a famous palace. She said they ²_____ it on their first day and she ³_____ really impressed by it.

ELLIE I've heard that Seville's a beautiful city.

SOFIA That's right. Lucy told me that she ⁴_____ lots of fascinating sights like the Giralda Tower and a beautiful square, Plaza de España.

ELLIE Where's she going next?

SOFIA She said they ⁵_____ to Cáceres next.

Verb patterns: object + infinitive

`SB p.107`

4 ★☆☆ **Match the sentence halves.**

0 They said the mountain was dangerous and **[f]**

1 She invited us to stay at their ☐

2 I was very tired, but John ☐

3 The tickets were expensive, but they ☐

4 Logan is a great footballer. They picked ☐

5 It'll be cold tonight, so Joanne reminded me to ☐

6 I'm not too sure about my Spanish, but my ☐

7 Mr Miller told us to study harder, and we ☐

a persuaded me to stay up for a few more hours.

b allowed us to get in without queuing.

c him to play in the school's all-star team.

d bring some warm clothes.

e teacher always encourages me to speak in class.

f warned us not to climb it without a good guide.

g asked him to explain the grammar again.

h place for the weekend.

5 ★★★ **Complete the conversations. Use the correct patterns of the verbs in brackets.**

0 A What did Jacob want from you?
 B Oh, he __wanted me to help__ (want / help) him in the garden.

1 A Why didn't you take the four o'clock bus, guys?
 B Our friends _____ (persuade / stay) a bit longer.

2 A I've heard you aren't coming to the park with us.
 B No. Mum _____ (ask / help) her with the shopping.

3 A Why didn't you watch the film at home?
 B Our neighbours _____ (invite / watch) it on their big screen.

4 A Why aren't you coming into the garden?
 B Well, my friends have _____ (warn / not get) too close to your dog.

5 A Is Carol a good swimmer?
 B Yes. They've just _____ (pick / be) the captain of the school team.

6 A Your sister came second in the race!
 B Yes, that's right. I _____ (not expect / do) so well.

7 A Why didn't Jack go out on Thursday night?
 B His parents _____ (not allow / go out) except at the weekend.

Pronunciation

Polite intonation

Go to page 121. 🔊

6 **Rewrite the sentences. Say what happened. Use the verb in brackets.**

0 Sally: 'Jon, would you like to see a film?' (invite)
 Sally invited Jon to see a film.

1 Pauline: 'Mary, can you help me please?' (ask)
 _____

2 Dave: 'You should join the band, Mia.' (encourage)
 _____

3 Andy: 'Meet me at six o'clock, Paul.' (tell)
 _____

4 Mr Jones: 'Jack! Don't go into the sea!' (warn)
 _____

5 Mike's Dad: 'Don't forget to feed the dog, Mike.' (remind)
 _____

7 ★★★ **Complete the conversations. Use the verbs in brackets to disagree.**

0 A Here are your steaks. (ask)
 B But _I asked you to buy some vegetables!_

1 A You did Exercise 2. That's wrong. (tell)
 B But _____

2 A I forgot your DVDs. (remind)
 B But _____

3 A He fell out of the tree and broke his leg. (warn)
 B But _____

4 A You didn't come to my party! (not invite)
 B But _____

GET IT RIGHT!

Verb tenses with *ask*, *say* and *tell*

Learners sometimes use the wrong tenses with *ask*, *say* and *tell*.

✓ I **told** her I could help.

✗ I *tell* her I could help.

Correct the following sentences.

0 When I heard the news, I ask if it was true.
 When I heard the news, I asked if it was true.

1 She says she'd call me yesterday, but she didn't.
 _____

2 We invited Ben and tell him to bring pizza.
 _____

3 I am so happy that you ask me to write the article.
 _____

4 Tomorrow I ask a friend about the homework.
 _____

5 Dan, I already tell them that you're coming tonight.
 _____

VOCABULARY

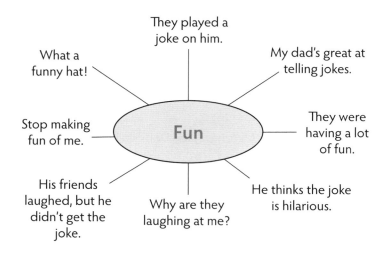

More verbs with object + infinitive

persuade   expect
encourage   remind
warn   allow
invite   pick

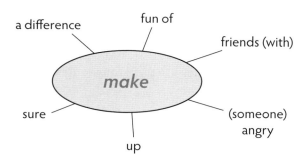

Key words in context

blizzard	A **blizzard** is a heavy snow storm.
candidate	There were 12 **candidates** in the show, but Leah was by far the best.
crop	The potato **crop** was very good last year.
escape	The situation was very dangerous, but they managed to **escape**.
expert	Luca's mum is a top computer **expert**. She knows everything about them.
floods	It had rained heavily and we couldn't get into the town because of the **floods**.
hailstorm	We were caught in a **hailstorm**; frozen lumps of ice fell from the sky.
lucky break	He was unsuccessful as a photographer for a long time, but he got a **lucky break** when one of his photos was chosen for the cover of a top magazine.
tornado	The **tornado** blew the roof off our house.

More personality adjectives SB p.102

1 ★ ☆ ☆ **Complete the definitions.**

0 A _talented_ person is very good at something.

1 An i_____ person understands things easily.

2 A c_____ person believes in him- or herself.

3 A w_____ person is friendly and loving.

Fun SB p.104

2 ★★ ☆ **Complete the conversations with 'fun' words.**

0 A Why can't you go to the office like this?
   B Everybody will _laugh at me._

1 A Hahahaha!
   B It isn't _____ . Stop laughing, please.

2 A Did you enjoy the birthday party?
   B Oh, yes. It was such good _____ .

3 A I didn't like the film at all.
   B I thought it was _____ . I couldn't stop laughing.

4 A Why doesn't Anna want to go to school?
   B The other kids _____ of her because she wears glasses.

5 A I didn't _____ .
   B I know what you mean. It's never easy to understand jokes in another language.

6 A Jane's really good at telling _____ .
   B Yes, she always makes me laugh.

7 A Shall we play a _____ on Dad?
   B Yes! Let's hide his newspaper.

More verbs with object + infinitive
SB p.107

3 ★★ ☆ **Match the sentence halves.**

1 I warned them not to ☐
2 My English teacher picked me to ☐
3 I wasn't expecting you to be home ☐
4 My parents don't allow my little sister to ☐
5 He's very shy. I think we should encourage ☐
6 Can I remind you to buy ☐
7 Can we invite you to come ☐

a him to play the piano at the school concert.
b watch TV at all. They think it's bad for her.
c to our place on Saturday?
d read out a story to the whole class.
e so early.
f be late.
g some vegetables for lunch?

4 ★★ ☆ **Put the letters in order.**

0 Farmers are predicting a good _crop_ (orpc).

1 That _____ (aodtrno) looks dangerous.

2 A _____ (oalrmhsti) broke our greenhouse.

3 We had to _____ (aseecp) through a window.

4 He is an _____ (reeptx) on Shakespeare.

5 There was a _____ (zarzlidb) in the mountains.

6 The best _____ (ntddicaae) will get the job.

WordWise SB p.109
Expressions with *make*

5 ★ ☆ ☆ (Circle) **the correct words.**

0 This story is too good to be true. I'm sure they made it *off* / (up) / *on* / *down*.

1 Let me make *good* / *fun* / *easy* / *sure* I understand.

2 He didn't even apologise. That made us really *angry* / *cool* / *easy* / *worse*.

3 Good teachers can make a *desire* / *distance* / *damage* / *difference* to students' lives.

4 I know her, but I've never made *students* / *friends* / *partners* / *colleagues* with her.

5 Don't make *jokes* / *fun* / *laughter* / *play* of me.

6 ★★ ☆ **Match the questions with the replies.**

0 Shall we do that now or tomorrow? [d]
1 Can I borrow £10? ☐
2 Why don't you like them? ☐
3 What did you think of the book? ☐
4 Is this really what happened? ☐
5 When did you make friends? ☐

a OK, but make sure you pay me back.
b Because they make fun of me all the time.
c Of course not. They made it up.
d You choose. It makes no difference to me.
e A long time ago. We went to school together.
f It made me really happy.

7 ★★★ **Answer the questions.**

1 What makes you angry?
   _____

2 Have you ever read a news story that was made up?
   _____

3 Does sport make a difference to your life?
   _____

READING

1 REMEMBER AND CHECK **Answer the questions. Then check your answers in the article on page 102 of the Student's Book.**

0   How did people react to the BBC story about Swiss farmers and their spaghetti crop?
Many people believed the story and wanted to know how they could grow their own spaghetti.

1   Why do many reporters seem to like the opportunity to fool people once a year?

_____

2   What did the BBC say about penguins once?

_____

3   What was 'special' about Edison's food machine?

_____

4   What did the Daily Mail say about a Japanese runner?

_____

5   What did the owner of a restaurant claim about their hamburgers?

_____

2   Read the article quickly. What happened in April 2013?

_____

Too good to be true – fake Harry Potter news story fools everyone

When fans all over the world read on social media that J.K. Rowling was working on a new Harry Potter book, it sounded so good that they decided to believe it. Unfortunately, it was too good to be true. But it was too late – the story had already made the rounds on social media.

It all happened in 2013, when an April Fool's joke claimed that Rowling was working on the eighth novel in the series and had already written about three quarters of the book. The new book, the news said, would continue where *Harry Potter and the Deathly Hallows* had finished.

What people didn't notice (or maybe didn't want to notice because they were so looking forward to another novel by their hero!) was the date of the original message – 1st April!

Maybe what also made it difficult for fans to notice that the story wasn't true was that it gave various details, saying, for example, that there might be a ninth film in the series based on the new book. And the message said, 'While none of the series' actors have officially signed on, one of the stars has already voiced his excitement about returning to play the title role.' And then, of course, there was even a (false!) quote by Daniel Radcliffe, saying, 'When we wrapped up the last film, I still felt like I wasn't finished with this grandiose story. I can't wait to come back.'

Rowling and her new Harry Potter book are not the only example of a news story that was totally made up. The history of the media is full of such stories, and since the beginning of the Internet, the number of news stories and the speed at which they get passed on around the globe has increased enormously. But what is it that makes it possible for so many people to become the victims of false stories? Well, first of all, many people don't read critically enough. They believe everything they read, see or hear in the media. And quite often it's also because they want to believe something – because it sounds so good, like the story of J.K. Rowling's new Harry Potter book!

3   Read the article again. Complete the sentences using no more than three words.

0   Fans believed that J.K. Rowling *was working* on a new book.

1   The story was first released on 1st _____ .

2   The story gave various _____ too and maybe that made it difficult to notice it was false.

3   The message also had a quote by the Harry Potter actor, but it too was _____ .

4   There have always been false stories in the _____ .

5   People often do not read _____ enough.

6   They often believe what they read, _____ in the media.

7   And quite often they believe what they _____

DEVELOPING WRITING

A report for the school magazine

1 Read the report quickly. What do the numbers refer to?

0 1997 *The year the Guggenheim Museum was created.*

1 11,000 _____

2 4a _____

3 24,000 _____

⊖ ☐ ✕

The day we visited a museum – in cyber space!

A For the students in Class 4a of our school, the English lessons in the first week of this month were very different from what we normally do. We were pretty excited when Mr Breen, our teacher, told us to choose a museum in a different country and 'visit' it (via the Internet, of course) together in groups. He also said that we should write an article for the school magazine about it.

B There were five of us in my group, and it wasn't easy to decide which museum we wanted to go to. Mr Breen encouraged us to make one suggestion each. We were surprised how easy it was. We had five suggestions, but everybody was very impressed with Thomas's idea. He wanted us to visit the Guggenheim Museum in Bilbao in the north of Spain, and when he showed us the website, we all knew it was 'our place'.

C The building was created by American architect Frank Gehry in 1997, and it's amazing. The website says it covers an area of 24,000 m², of which 11,000 m² are all exhibition space. It took us about two hours to visit the different parts of the website, and we all loved the photos of the building. The part we liked best was called Explore. It shows really attractive photos of sculptures and other pieces of art from the different exhibitions.

D When the project was finished, Mia, one girl from our group, summed up how we all felt. She said that the project had been fascinating, but what we'd really like to do now is visit the Guggenheim in Bilbao!

Mark Steyn, 14, 4a

2 Complete the sentences from the report with the missing verb forms.

1 Our teacher told us _____ a museum in a different country.

2 Thomas _____ the group to visit the Guggenheim.

3 Mia said the project _____ fascinating, but what we _____ really like to do now is visit the Guggenheim in Bilbao.

Writing tip: reported speech

- When you write a news story, it's a good idea to use reported speech because it helps you to sum up the most important things that someone said, and you don't need to write down everything they said word for word.

- In the text above, for example, the writer says this about Mia: *She said that the project had been fascinating.* This is most probably a summary – Mia might have said much more here, but it isn't important to say that word for word.

3 Read the text again. Match the descriptions with the paragraphs.

0 This paragraph talks about how the students liked the event (their 'visit' to the museum). ☐ D

1 This paragraph tells the story of how the students decided which museum to visit. ☐

2 This paragraph is about what was different from a 'normal week' for the students. ☐

3 This paragraph describes the place and gives details about it. ☐

4 Plan a report for your school magazine.

- What do you want to write about? (For example, an event at school? A school fair? A special ceremony? A fancy dress party?)

- What are the important details of the event – time, place, people? What happened?

- How did people react? What interesting comments were there?

5 Write your report (about 200 words).

LISTENING

1 🔊45 **Listen to the conversations. Match them with the types of problems.**

a   relationship problems ☐

b   an environmental problem ☐

c   someone not feeling good about themselves ☐

2 🔊45 **Listen again and answer the questions.**

CONVERSATION 1

0   Where are Andrew and Elizabeth?
   They're in a park.

1   Why is Andrew cross?

2   What does Andrew think the police should do?

CONVERSATION 2

3   How does Anna feel about joining the club?

4   What happened at her old school?

5   How does Sam feel about what the boy said?

CONVERSATION 3

6   Why is Max upset?

7   What does Layla think he should do?

8   Why can't Max do that?

3 🔊45 **Match the statements and responses. Then listen again and check.**

1   What's up? | a |

2   I get really cross when I see something like this. ☐

3   He always said I was a hopeless actor. ☐

4   What really counts is that you enjoy what you do and want to become better. ☐

5   How do you know Ian's telling the truth? ☐

6   But I can't go and ask Ian ☐

a   Just look at the mess over there.

b   Me too. This is awful.

c   That's right. You know what? I think I'll give it a try and join the club.

d   I don't. But I can't go and ask Ian.

e   Seriously? I get so angry when people say things like that.

f   Why not?

DIALOGUE

1 **Put the conversation in the correct order.**

☐ DYLAN   But just imagine if that really worked! I think I'll ask my Science teacher about it.

☐ DYLAN   I'm just saying I'll talk to my Science teacher. Don't shout at me.

1 DYLAN   Hey, Emma, check this out. The paper says this guy has just discovered how to produce petrol from nothing.

☐ EMMA   I'm telling you – it's not worth it. It's all complete nonsense.

☐ EMMA   From nothing? I think we're talking about news that's made up.

☐ EMMA   Sorry, I didn't mean to be rude. Of course you can have a word with your Science teacher. See what she thinks.

(2 hours later)

☐ DYLAN   She was like, 'You shouldn't believe everything you see in a newspaper!'

☐ DYLAN   Yeah, I know.

☐ EMMA   See? I told you.

☐ EMMA   So what did she say?

PHRASES FOR FLUENCY

1 **Complete the conversations with the expressions in the list.**

was like | have a word | I'm just saying
check this out | we're talking about | it's not worth it

0   A   How did she react when she heard she'd won first prize?
   B   She *was like* , 'Me? I can't believe it's true!'

1   A   I said sorry to Anne, but she ignored me.
   B   Yes,_____. She never forgives anyone.

2   A   _____. It's a message I got this morning.
   B   Strange. Who would write something like this?

3   A   I'm angry with Steve. I'm not inviting him to my party.
   B   But_____ your best friend. Maybe you should have a chat with him.

4   A   Do you really need another piece of pizza?
   B   Yes, I do. Anyway, why are you so interested?
   A   _____ you've had enough.

5   A   Joanne seems upset and I don't know why.
   B   I think you should_____ with her after school.

Help with reading: guessing the meaning of words

- When you read a text, there will often be words that you haven't met before. If these words are important, and you can't use a dictionary (for example, because that would take too much time or because you're doing an exam and aren't allowed to use one), you'll need to try to guess the meaning from the context.

- N.B. If a word isn't important for the understanding of the text, just carry on reading.

Tip: guessing the meaning of words

- To start, it's a good idea to decide what part of speech the word is. Look at the position in the sentence, and its ending. If, for example, it ends in *-ed* or *-ing*, it might be a verb or an adjective. If it ends in *-s*, it might be a plural noun (or a verb in the 3rd person singular, of course).

- When you know what part of speech it is, look at other words around the unknown word. If it's a noun, is there an article? If it's an adjective, is there a noun that goes with it? If it's a verb, is there an object?

- Look around in the same sentence or in the sentences around it. Are there any small words (*but, so, however, and*) that help you with the meaning? Take, for example, the sentence *When he reached the mountain top, he was happy but exhausted.* Imagine you don't know what *exhausted* means, but you know it's an adjective. The word *but* suggests that it means something very different from *happy*. You know from the first part of the sentence that he has just climbed a mountain, so a good guess would be that *exhausted* relates to that. You can probably guess that because it was a difficult climb, he was very happy, but very tired.

- Sometimes, the form of the word itself can help you, too. For example, you know that *impossible* means 'not possible' (the prefix *im-* often makes the meaning of an adjective negative). If you know this and you come across the word *imperfect,* you can easily guess what it means.

- When you've used the steps above and made a guess, read on to see if your guess seems correct. If not, and the word is really important, go back and do the steps again.

1 **Read the sentences and try to guess the meaning of the underlined words. Then (circle) the correct option: A, B or C.**

0 He was quite good-looking, but he had a <u>mole</u> on his nose which didn't look nice at all.
   A a kind of beard
   (B) a small black spot on the skin
   C a lot of blood

1 Sarah reads lots of books about illnesses. This has helped to <u>deepen</u> her understanding of the human body.
   A depend on something
   B make something deeper
   C become healthier

2 I haven't got his phone number, and it isn't in the <u>directory</u>.
   A a cupboard for books and small objects
   B a bag ladies often take with them to carry small things, such as car keys
   C a book that gives a list of names, addresses or other facts

3 I ordered the new laptop online at 9 pm and I was surprised when they <u>delivered</u> it the next morning.
   A repaired
   B took it back
   C brought it to my house

4 The weather will <u>dictate</u> what we do tomorrow.
   A decide or control what happens
   B stop something from happening
   C make an event impossible

5 Josephine is doing an excellent job for her company, so soon she will be <u>appointed</u> director of the new office in Paris.
   A previously, some time ago
   B excellent, one of the best
   C chosen for a job

6 I thought I had lost my pen, but one day it <u>turned up</u> in my mum's car, under the seat.
   A got lost
   B jumped
   C reappeared

7 The house looked beautiful from the outside, so we were surprised to see how <u>shabby</u> the furniture was.
   A untidy, in a bad condition
   B luxurious, very expensive
   C modern

GRAMMAR

be allowed to / let SB p.112

1 ★☆☆ **Match the sentences with the pictures.**

0 They don't let you play ball games here. `C`

1 You're allowed to swim here. ☐

2 You aren't allowed to use your phone here. ☐

3 They rode their bikes, but they weren't allowed to. ☐

4 You aren't allowed to swim here. ☐

5 They let their dogs run on the grass, but they aren't allowed to. ☐

2 ★☆☆ **Complete the sentences with *let(s)* or *allowed*.**

0 Mum ____*lets*____ me help her when she cooks.

1 I'm not _____ to go to parties on weekdays.

2 Are you _____ to watch TV every day?

3 My parents don't _____ me have a pet.

4 Does your dad _____ you drive his car?

5 I'm _____ to use my parents computer.

3 ★★☆ **Look at the information about Jason's school. Write the rules using *let* or *allowed*.**

OK!	NOT OK!
● wearing trainers	● eating during lessons
● forgetting homework once a month	● running in corridors
● sending work by email	● using phones in class
● using tablets	● borrowing more than three books from the library

0 *Students are allowed to wear trainers.*

1 The teachers let them _____

2 _____

3 _____

4 _____

5 _____

6 _____

7 _____

4 ★★☆ **Complete the conversation. Use *be allowed to* or *let* and the verbs in the list.**

~~do~~ | make | get | change | listen
chew | call | take | use | take

OLIVER So how do you like it here, Chloë?

CHLOE It's OK, but it's different from my old school.

OLIVER You mean you 0 *aren't allowed to do* things that you could do at your old school?

CHLOE Well, not really, but the rules are different. At my old school, we 1 _____ mobiles into the classroom, but here it's OK.

OLIVER Oh, I see. Well, they 2 _____ us _____ mobiles to check things online, but we 3 _____ calls.

CHLOE Oh, I see. 4 _____ they _____ us _____ someone at break?

OLIVER Sure, that's no problem.

CHLOE And do they 5 _____ us _____ to music in class?

OLIVER Of course not.

CHLOE The teachers at my old school 6 _____ us _____ MP3 players into class.

OLIVER Wow! That's amazing!

CHLOE And they 7 _____ us _____ gum.

OLIVER I should ask my parents to 8 _____ me _____ to your old school!

5 ★★★ **Write sentences about what you are or aren't allowed to do at school.**

Pronunciation

Silent consonants

Go to page 121. 🔊

Third conditional `SB p.115`

6 ★★☆ **Match texts 0–5 with sentences a–f.**

0 We were the better team, and the score was 2–1 to us. We had another three minutes to play, and I was so nervous. Then I caught the ball with my hands, right in front of our goal!

1 My mum told me I should be careful with my money. But I didn't think. I spent it all on sweets, and after a week it was all gone.

2 I was three years old. I knew I wasn't allowed to climb the ladder in my granddad's garden. But I did, and I had a bad accident.

3 They were late for the train. They ran as fast as they could, but missed it and had to wait for two hours.

4 It was awful. I didn't want to hurt Pat, but I was so stressed out. She asked me if I could help her, and I gave her a very unfriendly answer.

5 I'm sorry that I woke you up, Lily. I didn't know you were ill.

a If they'd started earlier, they wouldn't have got home so late. ☐

b I'd have been friendlier if I'd been more relaxed. ☐

c He wouldn't have broken his leg if he hadn't done that. ☐

d If he hadn't touched the ball with his hands, his team would have won. `0`

e If she'd listened, she wouldn't have bought all those sweets. ☐

f She wouldn't have rung her so early if somebody had told her about the situation. ☐

7 ★★☆ **Complete the sentences with the correct form of the verbs.**

0 If I had started to play the piano a few years ago, I _would have played_ (play) at the concert.

1 If I _____ (read) my emails this morning, I'd have answered you straight away.

2 If it had been warmer, they _____ (eat) in the garden.

3 We _____ (not lose) our way if the satnav had worked.

4 If I _____ (not study) so much, I wouldn't have written a good test.

5 Would you have lost the match if you _____ (not be) so nervous?

6 He _____ (not buy) the bike if the price hadn't been so low.

7 If Mia's friends had phoned her, she _____ (join) them?

8 ★★★ **Write third conditional sentences.**

0 On Sunday it was raining, so Terry got up late.
   If it hadn't been raining, Terry wouldn't have got up late.

1 He didn't hear the phone. Dan didn't talk to him.
   _____

2 Terry was on his own all afternoon. He was bored.
   _____

3 He went to bed at 6 pm. He woke up at midnight.
   _____

4 He didn't go back to sleep. He was tired on Monday.
   _____

5 He was tired. He found the Maths test difficult.
   _____

6 Terry got a bad mark. His teacher was disappointed.
   _____

9 ★★★ **Write true third conditional sentences.**

0 _If I'd caught the bus, I'd have been on time._

1 If I hadn't _____

2 If I'd _____

3 If I hadn't _____

GET IT RIGHT!
Third conditional

Learners sometimes use the wrong tenses in the third conditional – either in the main clause or in the _if_ clause.

✓ What **would have happened** if I hadn't been here?

✗ What ~~had happened~~ if I hadn't been here?

✓ If I **had seen** him, I would have said hello.

✗ If I ~~would have seen~~ him, I would have said hello.

Correct the following sentences.

0 If you hadn't helped me, I won't finish my essay.
   _____

1 If you'd have been there, it would have been fun.
   _____

2 The trip would have been difficult if it would rain.
   _____

3 It was worse if we hadn't got there on time.
   _____

4 I'm sure you would have enjoyed it if you were there.
   _____

5 If I hadn't brought my umbrella, I'd get wet.
   _____

VOCABULARY

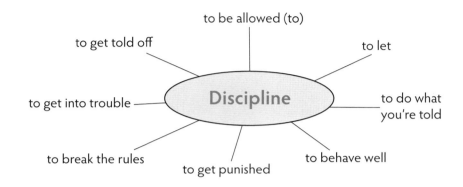

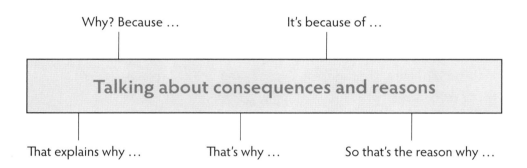

Key words in context

abandoned	No one lives in that old house any more.
break the law	He went to prison because he **broke the law**.
ceremony	There was a special **ceremony** to open the new museum.
crime	Stealing is a **crime**.
defeat	We lost 4–0. It was our worst **defeat** for two years.
end up	If you aren't careful, you'll **end up** having an accident.
except	The museum is open every day **except** Mondays.
illegal	It's **illegal** to park on this side of the road.
own	They **own** that attractive house down by the river.
prison	People who steal end up in **prison**.
punishment	His **punishment** was a month in prison.
slave	I saw a documentary about **slaves** in the US in the 19th century.
upside down	The answers are at the bottom of the page, **upside down**.
weave	They used sheep's wool to **weave** this blanket.

Discipline `SB p.112`

1 ★☆☆ **Complete the sentences with the phrases in the list.**

~~allowed to~~ | gets into trouble | let
breaks the rules | gets told off | do what they are told
gets punished | behave well

0 When you're *allowed to* do
something, you get permission to do it.

1 When your teachers don't _____
you do something, you can't do it without getting
into trouble.

2 When people _____, they do
what's expected of them.

3 When young children _____,
they act in a way that pleases other people.

4 When someone _____, they feel
the consequences of what they've done.

5 When someone _____, they're
doing something wrong.

6 When someone _____, they're
in a difficult situation.

7 When someone _____, another
person speaks angrily to them.

2 ★★☆ **Complete the conversations with the phrases in Exercise 1. Use the correct form of the verbs and make any other necessary changes.**

0 A Did the thief *get punished* ?
  B Yes, of course. He'll be in prison for three years.

1 A Did your brother _____ you borrow
    his tablet?
  B No. I took it without asking him.

2 A What was that shouting?
  B Jim _____ by Dad because he ran
    into the living room with dirty shoes on.

3 A Are you _____ use your dad's
    computer without asking?
  B No. I always have to ask first.

4 A Why can't I see Tommy any more?
  B Because you always _____ when
    you're with him.

5 A Your little sister is so nice. Does she always
    _____ ?
  B Only when she's with other people. Otherwise
    she can be a pain.

6 A Nadia, go and do your homework.
  B Mum, can I go out and do it tomorrow?
  A No, Nadia. _____ !

3 ★★★ **Complete the sentences so they are true for you.**

1 When I behave well, _____
  _____

2 My parents never let me _____
  _____

3 I always get told off when I _____
  _____

4 If you break the school rules, _____
  _____

5 When I get into trouble, I _____
  _____

6 I'm only allowed to _____

Talking about consequences and reasons `SB p.115`

4 ★☆☆ **Match the sentences.**

0 Last summer was the hottest one ever. `g`
1 You forgot Helen's birthday yesterday. ☐
2 I didn't get any sleep last night. ☐
3 So you're working late tonight? ☐
4 Sandra broke her leg two days ago. ☐
5 Tom got into trouble at school. ☐
6 I just don't have any money. ☐

a That explains why you're in such a bad mood today.
b Yes. It was because of his bad behaviour.
c That explains why she hasn't been at school.
d So that's why you don't want to come shopping
  with me.
e Yes, and that's why I can't join you for dinner.
f So that's the reason why she isn't talking to me.
g It's definitely because of global warming.

5 ★★★ **Complete the sentences so that they are true for you.**

1 I'm learning English because _____
  _____

2 _____
  because of the weather.

3 This weekend I've got to _____
  and that's why _____

4 Where I live, most people _____
  and that explains why _____

READING

1 REMEMBER AND CHECK (Circle) the correct words. Then check your answers in the article on page 111 of the Student's Book.

0   In Ancient Greece, babies weren't thought to be real people until they'd been alive for *three* / (*five*) days.

1   Parents who didn't want their babies just left them somewhere *outside* / *inside*.

2   Girls *were* / *weren't* allowed to go to school.

3   Girls stayed at home and were taught how to *weave* / *read* by their mothers.

4   At an early age, some boys were sent to a very *strict* / *strange* military school.

5   Boys were trained how to become *soldiers* / *slaves*.

6   The children of the Aztecs didn't really have *an easy* / *a difficult* life.

7   The rules for young people were very strict. If they broke them, they could get some nasty *surprises* / *punishments*.

2 Look at the photo. How do you think these children's experience of school was different from yours?

3 Read the article and check your answers.

Playing by the rules ... at schools

Most teachers these days will work very hard to have a good relationship (**A**). They encourage their students to say honestly what they like and don't like (**B**), and often teachers and students discuss together what they can do to make sure both get the most out of their time at school.

This wasn't always the case, and many of today's children would have quite a shock if they suddenly found themselves in a school a few hundred years ago. Unless they (**C**), of course!

In the old days, people believed that teachers had to be very strict and had the right to hit children. In the 19th century, hitting boys and girls with a bamboo stick – the 'cane' – (**D**) . It was used in both primary and secondary schools. Parents didn't mind if teachers beat their children when they didn't do what they'd been told to do. Often, the stricter a teacher was, the more parents thought he or she was a good teacher.

This may all sound really strange today, but let's imagine you'd gone to school in the 20th century. If you'd (**E**), how would your teachers have reacted? Well, they'd have hit you with a wooden ruler, and often also with a shoe, the branches of a tree, a wooden spoon or a hairbrush! Some children were also punished with cold water. Teachers either forced them to (**F**) – especially in countries with very cold winters – or lazy children sometimes had their head put into a bucket of cold water. And, of course, teachers told their students off all the time. Schools were often so strict that students were never ever allowed (**G**) unless the teacher had asked them a question!

Things didn't change until the middle of the 20th century or, in some countries, towards the end. Then beating children at school wasn't allowed any more. Of course, if teachers hit children these days, they'd be breaking the law and would (**H**) in most countries around the world.

4 Read the article again. Match the phrases with the correct places (A–H).

0   broken the rules   `E`

1   behaved very well   ☐

2   have a cold shower   ☐

3   with their students   ☐

4   be in trouble   ☐

5   was very common   ☐

6   to say a word   ☐

7   about their lessons   ☐

5 Mark the sentences T (true) or F (false).

0   Most modern schools encourage students to think about how they are educated.   `T`

1   The cane was used to punish students who didn't behave well.   ☐

2   A hundred years ago, strict teachers weren't popular with parents.   ☐

3   Water was sometimes used as a punishment.   ☐

4   Students were never allowed to speak in the classroom.   ☐

5   In most countries these days, teachers aren't allowed to use the cane.   ☐

DEVELOPING WRITING

A (light-hearted) set of rules

1 Read the rules. What is the punishment if you break any of them?

My 'dream' rules for the shopping mall

1 The main purpose of the Arcade Shopping Mall is for students to have a good time. Nobody is allowed to do anything that young people wouldn't like.

2 If a student is tired or hungry, they're allowed to go to a café and they can eat and drink whatever they want without paying. If no seats are free, an adult has to stand up so a young person can sit down.

3 Nobody is allowed to tell young people not to run around or use their skateboards in the corridors of the shopping mall. As soon as a young person is seen on a skateboard, all the adults have to go quickly into the shops and stay there until the skateboarder has left.

4 Whenever a young person goes into a shop, the shopkeeper has to ask the young person within one minute what music they want to hear. If the shopkeeper hasn't got the music the young person wants to hear, the young person can choose anything for free from the shop.

5 If young people don't like the clothes they find in a shop, shopkeepers aren't allowed to keep those clothes in the shop.

6 Anyone who doesn't keep to these rules has to learn them by heart!

Writing tip: rules

- If you want to write a light-hearted set of rules, it's important that the content is humorous and not serious.
- You can do that by writing the opposite of what the normal rules are. Can you find examples of that in the set of rules above?
- You can also make your set of rules sound more humorous if you exaggerate and make them sound particularly strict. For example: *Nobody is allowed to …*, *As soon as a young person is seen … , all the adults have to …, Everybody who doesn't keep to these rules has to … .*

2 Choose one of the situations and write sixlight-hearted rules. Use the ideas and the text in Exercise 1 to help you.

- Rules for the swimming pool (or sports ground, or any other place you frequently go to).
- An email to a student from another country who is going to visit your school, with rules for the school.
- Rules for your family and who has to do what in the house.

LISTENING

1 🔊47 **Listen to the conversations and match them with the pictures.**

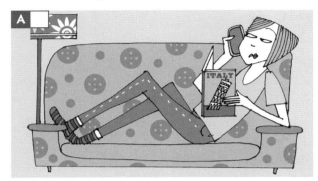

A ☐

B ☐

C ☐

2 🔊47 **Listen again. Write the two important rules in each situation.**

CONVERSATION 1

0 *Slow down when you see a sign showing a*
blue circle.

1 _____

_____

CONVERSATION 2

2 _____

_____

3 _____

_____

CONVERSATION 3

4 _____

_____

5 _____

3 **Complete the sentences with the words in the list.**

sign | disagree | slow down
ticket | referee | stamped

1 When you see the ___*sign*___ for a roundabout, you should _____ .

2 You need to put your _____ into a machine and get it _____ .

3 Never argue with the _____ or _____ with the coach.

DIALOGUE

1 **Put the conversation in the correct order.**

☐ **DEBBIE** Ticket validated? How do I do that?

☐ **DEBBIE** Sounds easy enough.

1 **DEBBIE** I'm so excited that I'm coming to visit you, but I'm a bit nervous about getting the train from Sistiana to Trieste. Is it very different from getting a train in the UK?

☐ **DEBBIE** OK – that's the same then.

☐ **GINO** Right. Just don't forget that. Otherwise you'll have to pay a fine.

☐ **GINO** Not really. The first thing you need to do is get a ticket. You can do that from the ticket window at the station, or from a machine.

☐ **GINO** But – and this is the important thing – you need to get your ticket validated.

☐ **GINO** Look for a yellow machine, and put your ticket into the machine. It stamps the ticket and that shows the date and the time of day. Now you're ready to go.

▰▰▰ TRAIN TO THiNK ▰▰▰

Create rules for a new country

1 **Imagine a new country has been discovered and you're going to be the ruler of it. Use the ideas to help you.**

- Where is it?
- Who is going to live there?
- What rules do you want to have?

2 **Write six rules for your new country.**

_____

_____

_____

_____

_____

_____

Help with listening: identifying individual words (2)

1 🔊 **48** **Listen and complete the text.**

We ⁰ _went_ to London at the weekend. We
¹_____ the train because it's quicker. We
²_____ all around the middle of the city – I think
we ³_____ ten kilometres! My parents wanted to
go to a museum, but I don't like ⁴_____ things, so I
asked if we ⁵_____ go to the London Eye instead.
They said OK, so that's what we did. We had a
⁶_____ time – I really ⁷_____ myself!

Tip: identifying individual words

- Something that's very important about spoken English is that there are often sounds (letters) that you don't hear.
- For example, take the sentence _We bought this old car last month._ It's really very difficult to pronounce the _t_ at the end of _bought_ because the next sound is _th_ (in the word _this_). So what do people do? They usually don't pronounce the _t_ in _bought_. And for the same kind of reason, a speaker would probably not say the _d_ in _old_ (because it's followed by the word _car_) or the _t_ in _last_ (because it's followed by the word _month_).

2 **Here are the missing words from Exercise 1. Listen to Exercise 1 again and see if you can hear the underlined letters.**

0	wen<u>t</u>	4	ol<u>d</u>
1	too<u>k</u>	5	coul<u>d</u>
2	walke<u>d</u>	6	grea<u>t</u>
3	walke<u>d</u>	7	enjoye<u>d</u>

Tip: reading and listening to English

Many people learning English find that it's very useful to read and listen to something at the same time – it can help you see how English is really spoken. So you can:

- listen to songs and read the words at the same time. You can usually finds the words (lyrics) of just about any song if you search for 'lyrics' plus the name of the song on the Internet.
- find readers (special books to help people who are learning English) that have a CD as well – then you can read and listen.
- watch films in English on DVD which have captions in English too – although be careful, because sometimes what you hear and what is written isn't 100 per cent the same!

3 🔊 **49** **Listen and complete the text.**

I ⁰ _went_ to town at the weekend and I ¹_____
three things. I ²_____ a new CD, but when I
³_____ to it, I didn't like it much. I ⁴_____ some
new trousers too – they ⁵_____ great! And the
⁶_____ thing I bought was a book about the
⁷_____ team in the world – my team!

CONSOLIDATION

LISTENING

1 🔊50 **Listen to the conversation.** (Circle) **the correct option: A, B or C.**

1 What time does the film start?

   A 7.30   **B** 7.40   **C** 7.45

2 What kind of film are they going to see?

   A sci-fi   **B** comedy   **C** action

3 Why can't they go in to see the film?

   A They aren't old enough.

   B The film has already started.

   C You can't enter after 8 o'clock.

2 🔊50 **Listen again. Answer the questions.**

0 How did Paul remind Jack about the film?

   He sent him a text message.

1 Why is Jack a bit late?

2 What will happen if Jack gets home after 11 pm?

3 What has Jack heard about the film?

4 What is the film called?

5 Where does Jack suggest they go when they can't see the film?

VOCABULARY

3 **Unscramble the letters and complete the sentences.**

~~neltatde~~ | ftonnicd | renugodeac

ebrka | edpushin | gellitnitn

0 She's a _talented_ singer with a great voice.

1 You'll be OK if you don't _____ the rules.

2 He's very _____ and learns quickly.

3 We were _____ if we did something wrong.

4 My friends _____ me to try bungee jumping.

5 She never thinks she can't do something – she's very _____ .

4 Complete the words.

0 They broke a window and got into a lot of _trouble_ with the neighbours.

1 Jack phoned me and r_____ me to take some music to his party.

2 Of course you're sick – I w_____ you not to drink that old milk.

3 I don't like him much because he m_____ fun of everyone.

4 We trained our dog and now he b_____ very well when we take him out.

5 He really didn't want to come with us at first, but in the end I p_____ him.

6 The teacher was angry with us – she really told us o_____ .

7 I was very surprised to hear that he lost the match – I e_____ him to win.

GRAMMAR

5 (Circle) **the correct words.**

0 She's such a good actress that they picked *to play* / (*her to play*) Juliet in *Romeo and Juliet*.

1 If *I'd known* / *I knew* you needed money yesterday, *I'd have lent* / *I lent* you some.

2 My parents always want *that I work* / *me to work* harder at school.

3 **A** John's coming to the party.

   B Really? Yesterday he said he *isn't* / *wasn't* coming.

4 He said he *didn't see* / *hadn't seen* the film before, so we went to see it last night.

5 We *would have arrived* / *have arrived* before midnight if we *would have left* / *had left* earlier.

6 **Complete the sentences. Use the correct form of *let* or *allow*.**

0 Our parents don't _let_ us play in the garden.

1 At school we aren't _____ to send text messages in lessons.

2 They didn't _____ me go in to see the film because I'm too young.

3 She never _____ her friends borrow her things.

4 Are you _____ to wear jeans to school?

5 If I hadn't got home on time, my parents wouldn't have _____ me to go out again.

DIALOGUE

7 Complete the conversation with the phrases in the list. There are two phrases you don't need.

~~was like~~ | have a word | I'm just saying | make sure | Check this out | made fun
We're talking about | it's not worth it | make it up | playing a joke

LOUISE You don't look very happy. What's wrong?

SALLY It's James Carter. He makes me so angry! I met him outside school and I said, 'Hi James!', and he ⁰ _was like_ 'Wow, Sally, tell me you didn't pay to have your hair cut like that!'

LOUISE What? ¹_____ James Carter here? He's one of the nicest guys at school.

SALLY Louise, I didn't ²_____ . That's exactly what he said. He ³_____ of me in front of my friends!

LOUISE OK, OK. Don't get angry with me too! ⁴_____ he's not usually rude.

SALLY Sorry, yes. It's just that I'm really, really upset!

LOUISE Look, why don't you calm down and then go and ⁵_____ with him? You know, you can ask him why he said it. And you can ⁶_____ he wasn't just trying to be funny.

SALLY No, I don't want to do that. I could talk to him, but ⁷_____ . He'll only say another unpleasant thing.

LOUISE OK, it's up to you. Come on, let's go and have lunch.

READING

8 Read the story. Answer the questions.

0 Why did the writer walk on the beach every day?
Because it helped him to relax, to get
ready for his working day, and to
get ideas

1 What was the weather like on that morning?
_____

2 What did the writer see the little girl doing when he was far away from her?
_____

3 Why was she throwing the starfish into the sea?
_____

4 Why did the writer think that she was wasting her time?
_____

5 Why did the girl think that she was making a difference?
_____

WRITING

9 Write a short story (about 150 words), true or made up, that ends with the words *It made a big difference to me.* (Instead of *me*, you could use *him / her / them / us*).

STARFISH

Once upon a time, there was a writer who had a house very close to the sea. Every morning, he went for a walk along the beach – it helped him to relax, to get ready for his working day, and to get ideas.

One beautiful sunny morning, as he was walking near the edge of the water, he looked along the beach and in the distance he saw a little girl near the water. She was bending down and then standing up – he wasn't sure what she was doing. So he decided to go closer to find out.

When he got near to the little girl, he saw that on the beach there were lots of starfish, and the little girl was picking them up, one at a time, and throwing them into the water.

The writer went closer to the girl and asked her what she was doing. The girl stopped and looked up at the writer – she seemed surprised. Then she said that she was throwing the starfish back into the sea. She said, 'The sun is up, and the tide is going out. If I don't throw the starfish back into the water, they'll die.'

Now it was the writer who was surprised. He wanted to persuade her that she was wasting her time. He said, 'But look, there are hundreds of starfish here. You can't possibly pick them all up and throw them back. It's not worth it. You can't possibly make a difference here.'

The girl looked at him, and said nothing. Then she picked up a starfish and threw it into the water. She turned to the writer and said, 'If I hadn't thrown it back, it would have died. So, I think I made a difference to that one.'

PRONUNCIATION

UNIT 1
Sentence stress

1 **Complete the sentences with the correct words from the list. Circle the stressed word in each sentence.**

~~brilliant idea~~ | a joke | to be famous one
changed forever | dangerous places | definitely do
fantastic time | is for living | had a terrible
help you | never heard | the new café

0 That's a ___*brilliant idea*___ !

1 Can I _____ ?

2 Then one day, her life _____ .

3 I know. Let's go to _____ !

4 We should _____ it!

5 We had a _____ .

6 She travels to some of the most _____ to take photos.

7 They're going _____ day.

8 Then my aunt _____ car accident.

9 I've _____ him complain.

10 'Life _____ ,' she said.

2 ◀))06 **Listen, check and repeat.**

UNIT 2
Word stress

1 **Write the verbs from the list in the correct columns.**

~~concentrate~~ | believe | forget | guess | know
think | recognise | remember | suppose

1 One syllable	2 Two syllables	3 Three syllables
_____	_____	*concentrate*
_____	_____	_____

2 ◀))07 **Listen, check and repeat.**

3 **Which syllable is stressed? Write the verbs in the correct columns.**

~~believe~~ | concentrate | consider | discuss
explain | imagine | listen | motivate
recognise | remember | study | wonder

Oo	oO	Ooo	oOo
_____	*believe*	_____	_____
_____	_____	_____	_____

4 ◀))08 **Listen, check and repeat.**

UNIT 3
Words ending with schwa /ə/

1 **Complete the sentences with comparative forms of the adjectives in the list.**

~~tidy~~ | early | funny | good
old | slow | tall | quiet

0 My sister's a lot ___*tidier*___ than me. Her bedroom is always clean.

1 There's too much noise here – let's go somewhere _____ .

2 He's very clever and much _____ at Maths than me.

3 Mum has to go to work at 8 o'clock; she gets up _____ than the rest of us.

4 My brother's 1.72 metres. He's _____ than me.

5 Jake's fourteen and his sister's ten. He's _____ than her.

6 You're driving too fast. Could you please go a little _____ ?

7 This comedy show is much _____ than the one we saw last week.

2 ◀))11 **Listen, check and repeat.**

3 Write the comparatives from Exercise 1 in the correct columns. <u>Underline</u> the stressed syllable. Remember that the final syllable 'er' is never stressed. It has the schwa /ə/ sound.

Two syllables	Three syllables
better	*earlier*

4 🔊12 Listen again, check and repeat.

UNIT 4
The short /ʌ/ vowel sound

1 Circle the word in each line that doesn't have the /ʌ/ sound (e.g. the sound in *son*, *one* and *done*).

	a		b		c		d	
0	a	son	b	one	c	done	d	(dog)
1	a	fun	b	won	c	home	d	come
2	a	shout	b	young	c	much	d	tongue
3	a	enough	b	cousin	c	you	d	love
4	a	must	b	mother	c	nose	d	doesn't
5	a	trouble	b	jump	c	other	d	note
6	a	love	b	stuff	c	funny	d	ground
7	a	put	b	wonder	c	under	d	nothing
8	a	could	b	some	c	lovely	d	brother
9	a	Sunday	b	Monday	c	over	d	cover
10	a	none	b	use	c	monkey	d	another
11	a	good	b	blood	c	touch	d	couple

2 🔊16 Listen, check and repeat.

UNIT 5
Strong and weak forms of *been* /biːn/ and /bɪn/

1 Match the statements (1–6) with the responses (a–g).

0 Have you <u>been</u> to London? __*e*__

1 Where have you been? You're covered in dirt!

_____

2 You look ill. _____

3 You need to go to the director's office, now. _____

4 Look at your face. It's so red! Where have you been? _____

5 How long has it been since you saw John? _____

6 The girls are tired. _____

a I know. I've been to the doctor's

b I've been working in the garden.

c It's been a long time – more than three months.

d They've been playing football.

e Yes, I have. I've been going there every summer since I was ten.

f I've been at the beach all day. I forgot my sun cream.

g I've already been.

2 🔊19 Listen, check and repeat.

3 Circle the strong forms of *been* /biːn/ and underline the weak forms of *been* /bɪn/.

4 🔊19 Listen again, check and repeat.

UNIT 6
/f/, /v/ and /b/ consonant sounds

1 🔊23 Listen and circle the word you hear.

0	a	(few)	b	view		3	a	ferry	b	very
1	a	fast	b	vast		4	a	leaf	b	leave
2	a	fan	b	van		5	a	off	b	of

2 🔊23 Listen, check and repeat.

3 Circle the correct words to complete the sentences.

0 They went out in Bill's dad's (boat) / *vote*.

1 That's a *berry* / *very* good idea.

2 She wants to be a *vet* / *bet* when she's older.

3 I wore my *best* / *vest* clothes to the party.

4 He drives a white *van* / *ban* for his job.

4 🔊24 Listen again, check and repeat.

UNIT 7
Intonation in question tags

1 🔊27 **Listen and draw ↗ when the voice goes up and ↘ when the voice goes down.**

Example 1 Your name's Lisa, isn't it? ↗
Example 2 You like chocolate, don't you? ↘

1 Tony hasn't been to Africa, has he?
2 Helen's in your sister's class, isn't she?
3 I haven't got any money, have I?
4 There's no milk left, is there?
5 You're Julie's cousin, aren't you?

2 🔊27 **Listen and check.**

3 **Tick (✓) the correct explanation (a or b) for each tag from Exercise 1.**

0 a I've met Lisa before. ✓
   b I'm not sure what this girl's name is. _____
00 a I'm surprised because you don't want any chocolate. _____
   b I know you like chocolate. ✓
1 a I know Tony hasn't been to Africa. _____
   b I'm surprised that Tony's been to Africa. _____
2 a I think Helen's in your sister's class. _____
   b I don't know if Helen's in your sister's class. _____
3 a I don't know if I have money or not. _____
   b I know I don't have any money. _____
4 a I wonder if there's any milk. _____
   b I don't think there's any milk. _____
5 a I don't know Julie. _____
   b I think you are Julie's cousin. _____

4 🔊27 **Listen, check and repeat.**

UNIT 8
The /juː/ sound

1 **Find the words with the /juː/ sound. There are ten words in total and they all appear in Unit 8.**

U	E	U	R	E	K	A	E	C	A
S	N	E	W	T	O	N	W	O	U
E	F	E	E	O	T	M	H	M	S
D	Z	R	W	R	C	U	O	P	U
I	A	O	W	T	R	U	R	U	A
I	F	U	T	U	R	E	R	T	L
Y	O	U	C	H	R	F	U	E	L
R	E	V	I	E	W	T	U	R	Y

2 🔊29 **Listen and check.**

3 **Circle the word that doesn't have the /juː/ sound.**

0 news (flew) nephew
1 music   student   umbrella
2 Tuesday   guess   statue
3 few   knew   threw
4 amusing   butter   nutrition

4 🔊30 **Listen, check and repeat.**

UNIT 9
/tʃ/ and /dʒ/ consonant sounds

1 **Complete the sentences with the correct word from the list below.**

chair | switch | charities | future
questions | match | chocolate

0 When she broke her leg, she had to use a wheel *chair*_____ .
1 Did you see the football final? It was an exciting _____ .
2 I'd like to travel the world in the _____ .
3 When she was younger, she worked as a _____ board operator.
4 There are many _____ to help children in need.

2 **Which one sound occurs in all of the words in the list in Exercise 1? Circle the sound in each word.**

3 🔊34 **Check your answer with the key. Then, listen and repeat.**

4 **Complete the sentences with the correct word from the list.**

changing | message | jokes | bridge
agent | join | dangerous

0 Many jobs are disappearing because the world is *changing*_____ so fast.
1 We're going to the new café. Would you like to _____ us?
2 We must cross that _____ to go over the river.
3 My best friend makes me laugh. She's always telling _____ .
4 If you can't come, just send me a text _____ .

5 **Which one sound occurs in all of the words in the list in Exercise 4? Circle the sound in each word.**

6 🔊35 **Check your answer with the key. Then, listen and repeat.**

UNIT 10
/tʃ/ and /ʃ/ consonant sounds

1 🔊39 **Who do you meet? Put your finger on** *Start.* **Listen to the words. Go up if you hear the** /tʃ/ **sound (e.g. chips) and down if you hear the** /ʃ/ **sound (e.g. ships). Say the word at the end.**

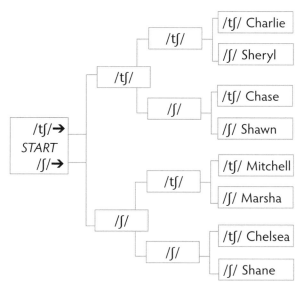

0   shoes – cheese – wish. Who do you meet?
    Marsha

1 _____   2 _____   3 _____   4 _____   5 _____

2 🔊39 **Listen again, check and repeat.**

3 🔊40 **Complete the sentences with the different spellings of the** /ʃ/ **sound. Listen and check.**

0   My sister loves fa _sh_ ion magazines.

1   I put my money in the ma _____ine but it didn't give me a can of cola!

2   I wi _____ I had a lot of money so I could buy that bike.

3   We're going to the beach now. Are you _____ure you don't want to come?

4   We can get all the informa_____ion we need at the train station.

4 🔊40 **Check your answers with the key. Then, listen and repeat.**

5 🔊41 **Write the words on the correct line. Then listen and check.**

~~future~~ | competition | conclusion | decision
delicious | mixture | passion | question | revision

/ʃ/ – fashion   _____   _____

/tʃ/ – picture   *future*   _____

/ʒ/ – television   _____   _____

UNIT 11
Polite intonation

1 **Where would you hear each of these statements or questions? Write A for airport, R for restaurant or C for classroom.**

2 🔊43 **Listen and put a tick (✓) if the speaker sounds polite. Put a cross (✗) if the speaker sounds rude.**

		Where?	Is it polite?
0	Put that suitcase over there.	A	✗
1	When does the plane leave?		
2	I don't understand the question, Mr Jones.		
3	Are you ready to order?		
4	Put up your hand if you know the answer.		
5	You arrive in London at half past eight.		
6	Have you got anything without cheese?		

3 🔊43 **Listen, check and repeat.**

4 🔊44 **Now the sentences are said politely. How is the speaker's voice different? Listen and repeat.**

UNIT 12
Silent consonants

1 **Underline the spelling mistakes. Write the correct spelling.**

0   That's the <u>rong</u> answer to this question. _*wrong*_

1   Her dauter's six and her name's Cynthia.

2   We played paper, sissors, rock in class yesterday.

3   Woud you like a drink of water?

4   My parents are taking me to an iland for our next holiday.

5   Our English class is an our long on Fridays.

6   I'm going to order the samon and salad. It looks good!

7   I asked her if she was okay, but she didn't anser me.

8   We musn't leave the classroom before the bell rings.

2 🔊46 **Listen and repeat.**

GRAMMAR REFERENCE

UNIT 1
Present perfect with *just*, *already* and *yet*

We often use the present perfect with the words *just / already / yet*.

1 We use *just* before the past participle to say that something happened a short time ago.
*They've **just** come back from their holiday.*

2 We use *already* at the end of a sentence or before the past participle to show surprise, or to emphasise that something has been done, or finished, sooner than expected.
*Have you finished **already**?*
*No food thanks – I've **already** eaten.*

3 We use *yet* at the end of negative sentences and questions, to emphasise that something hasn't happened but probably will in the future.
*Have you finished your homework **yet**?*
*I haven't played that game **yet** (but I will).*

Present perfect vs. past simple

1 We use the past simple to talk about events which are complete and finished, or 'before now', at the time of speaking.
*I **saw** you in town yesterday. Who **were** you with?*

2 We use the present perfect to connect the past and 'now' (at the time of speaking).
*I **haven't seen** you this week. Where **have** you **been**?*

UNIT 2
Present perfect with *for* and *since*

1 We can use the present perfect to talk about something that began in the past and continues to be true in the present.
*We**'ve lived** here for ten years (= and we still live here.)*

2 We talk about the time between when something started and now with *for* or *since*.
- We use the word *for* when we mention a period of time from the past until now.
for half an hour / for three months / for ages
- We use the word *since* when we mention a point in time in the past.
since six o'clock / since 2012 / since last weekend

a, an, the or no article

1 We use *a, an* before a singular, countable noun to talk about something for the first time in a conversation.
*Look – there's **a horse** in the garden!*
*Do you want **an apple**?*
We also use *a / an* when we are not talking about a specific thing.
*I haven't got **a** computer.*

2 We use *the* before a noun when it is clear which thing(s) or person/people we are talking about.
***The** apples in our garden are delicious.*
*Have you got **the** book? (= the book we were talking about before)*
***The** woman next door is really friendly.*
We also use the when there is only one thing that exists.
*Look at **the** moon!*

3 We use no article (zero article) before plural countable nouns, and before uncountable nouns, when we are talking about things in general.
***Cars** are expensive.*
***Love** is the most important thing.*

UNIT 3
Comparative and superlative adjectives (review)

1 When we want to compare two things, or two groups of things, we use a comparative form + *than*.
*My sister is **older than** me.*
*My old phone was **more expensive than** my new one.*
*The film is **better than** the book.*

2 With short adjectives, we normally add *-er*. With longer adjectives (more than two syllables), we normally don't change the adjective – we put *more* in front of it.

hot ➔ *hotter   short* ➔ *shorter   clever* ➔ *cleverer*
interesting ➔ ***more** interesting*
exciting ➔ ***more** exciting*

3 Some adjectives are irregular – they have a different comparative form.

good ➔ *better   bad* ➔ *worse   far* ➔ *further*

(not) as ... as

When we want to say that two things are the same (or not the same) we can use *(not) as* + adjective + *as*.

*She's **as tall as** her mother now.*
*This question isn**'t as easy as** the last one.*

Making a comparison stronger or weaker

We can make a comparison stronger or weaker by using *much / far, a lot* or *a little / a bit*. These words come before the comparison.

*His computer is **far better** than mine.*
*His bike was **much more expensive** than mine.*
*He lives **a little further** from school than I do.*

Adverbs and comparative adverbs

1 We use adverbs to describe verbs — they say how an action is or was performed.

*She <u>shouted</u> **angrily**. <u>Run</u> **quickly**!*
*They <u>got</u> to the theatre **early**.*
We can also use adverbs before adjectives.
*It was **really** <u>cold</u> on Sunday.*
*The coffee was **incredibly** <u>hot</u>, so I couldn't drink it.*

2 Most adverbs are formed by adjective + *-ly*.

slow ➔ *slowly   nice* ➔ *nicely*
If the adjective ends in *-le*, we drop the *-e* and add *-y*.
incredible ➔ *incredibly   possible* ➔ *possibly*
If the adjective ends in consonant + *-y* we change the *-y* to *-i* and add *-ly*.
angry ➔ *angrily   lucky* ➔ *luckily*
hungry ➔ *hungrily*

3 Some adverbs are irregular – they don't have an *-ly* ending.

good ➔ *well   fast* ➔ *fast   hard* ➔ *hard*
early ➔ *early   late* ➔ *late*

4 To compare adverbs, we use the same rules as we do when we compare adjectives. With short adverbs, we add *-er* or *-r*, and *than* after the adverb.

*I worked **hard**, but Sue worked **harder than** me!*

5 With longer adverbs, we use *more* (+ adverb) + *than*.

*She does things **more easily than** me.*

6 To compare the adverb *well*, we use *better ... than*. To compare the adverb *far*, we use *further ... than*.

*He cooks **better than** me.*
*London to Mumbai is **further than** London to New York.*

UNIT 4
Indefinite pronouns

1 We can use the words *every / some / no / any* together with *one / thing / where* to make compound nouns.

everyone = all the people
everything = all the things
everywhere = all the places
someone = a person, but we don't know who
something = a thing, but we don't know which
somewhere = a place, but we don't know where
no one = none of the people
nothing = none of the things
nowhere = none of the places
anyone = any person / any of the people
anything = any of the things
anywhere = any of the places

2 These words are all singular.

***Something smells** nice. **No one's** here. **Nothing was** found. **Everywhere was** full. **Someone has** opened my desk.*

3 We don't use negatives with *nothing* and *no one*. We use *anything* or *anyone* instead.

*I don**'t** know **anyone** here.*
(NOT I ~~don't know no one~~ here.)

all (some / none / any) of them

With other nouns and pronouns, we use *all of / some of / none of* + plural or uncountable noun/pronoun.

***All of** them are yours.   **Some of** the teachers are really nice.*
***None of** my friends called me yesterday.*
*Do **any of** you know the answer?*

should(n't), had better, ought to

1 *Should, had ('d) better* and *ought to* are all used to give advice.

2 *Should* and *ought to* both mean 'I think it's (not) a good idea for you/me/him (etc.) to do this'.

*You **should do** more exercise. (= I think it is a good idea for you to do more exercise.)*
*She **shouldn't talk** in class. (= I think it is not a good idea for her to talk in class.)*
*We **ought to** leave now. (= I think it is a good idea for us to leave now.)*

3 The meaning of *had better* is often stronger. The speaker wants to say that there are negative consequences if the person ignores the advice.

*I'd **better run**.* (or I'll be late)
*You'd **better not talk** in class.* (or the teacher will be angry)

4 *Should, had better* and *ought to* are all followed by the infinitive of another verb.

*You **should be** more careful.   I **ought to eat** more fruit.   We'd **better hurry** or we'll be late.*

5 *Should* and *had better* form the negative by adding *not* afterwards.

*They **shouldn't** be so rude.*
*We'd **better not** stay out late.*

> We make *ought to* negative by putting *not* after *ought* (but we don't use this form very often).

*You **ought not to** make so much noise.*

UNIT 5
Present perfect continuous

1 The present perfect continuous is formed with the present tense of *have + been +* the *-ing* form of the verb.

*I've **been reading** since breakfast.*
*Have you **been sitting** here all day?*

2 Sentences with the present perfect always connect the present and the past. We often use the present perfect continuous to talk about activities which started in the past and are still continuing now.

*She's **been running** for an hour.* (= She started running an hour ago, and she is still running.)

3 We also use the present perfect continuous to talk about actions with a result in the present. These actions may or may not be complete.

*I'm tired because I've **been working**.*
*Jack's feeling ill because he **hasn't been eating** well.*

4 We also use the present perfect continuous to talk about actions which began in the past and continue to the present, but perhaps we are not doing the action at the time of speaking.

*We've **been studying** Spanish for six months.*
(= We started studying six months ago, and we are still studying, but we're not studying at this exact moment.)

Present perfect simple vs. present perfect continuous

1 We use the present perfect simple to show that an action is finished, or to focus on what (and how much) we have completed in a period of time.

*I've **written** an email.*
*I've **written** twelve emails this morning.*

2 We use the present perfect continuous to show that an action is still going on, or to focus on how long something has been in progress.

*I've **been reading** this book for two days.*
*I've **been reading** detective stories for years.*

> **Compare the sentences:**
*She's **been writing** books for many years.*
*She's **written** over twenty books.*

UNIT 6
will (not), may (not), might (not) for prediction

1 We can use the modal verb *will ('ll)* or *will not (won't)* to make predictions about the future.

*Don't worry about the exam – it **won't be** difficult.*

2 We use *might/might not* or *may/may not* to make less certain predictions about the future.

*It **might rain** this afternoon – if it does, then I **may not** go the match.*

First conditional / *unless* in first conditional sentences

1 We use the first conditional to talk about possible actions / situations in the future, and their (possible) results.

If I finish my homework, I'll go out.

2 We often make conditional sentences by using *if + subject + present simple* in the *if* clause, and *will/won't / might/might not* in the main clause.

*If I **have** time this afternoon, I'**ll go** for a walk.*
*We **might go** out tonight if there's nothing good on TV.*

3 We can also use the word *unless* in conditional sentences – it means *if not*.

*She **won't come unless** you **ask** her.* (= She won't come if you don't ask her.)

4 There are two clauses in these sentences. We can put the main clause first, or the *if/unless* clause first. When the *if/unless* clause comes first, there is *a comma (,) after it*.

***Unless** you tell me, I won't know what to do.*
*I won't know what to do **unless** you tell me.*

UNIT 7
Future forms (review)

1 We often use the present simple to talk about fixed future events.

*My uncle is coming to visit us. His plane **arrives** at six o'clock tomorrow.*

2 We often use *be going to* to talk about future plans and intentions.

*I'm **going to be** a doctor when I grow up.*

3 We often use *will/won't* to make predictions about the future.

*Don't worry about her. I'm sure she**'ll be** OK.*

4 We often use the present continuous to talk about future arrangements.

*They**'re getting** married next June.*

Question tags

1 Question tags are positive or negative questions at the end of statements. We add 'tags' to the end of statements:

a) when we are not sure that what we are saying is correct, and we want the other person to say if we are correct or not.

b) when we are sure that what we are saying is correct, and we want the other person to say something about it.

2 Tags in (a) above have a rising intonation pattern.

A: *You're Spanish, aren't you?* ↗
B: *No, I'm not. I'm Mexican.*

Tags in (b) above have a falling intonation pattern.

A: *You're Spanish, aren't you?* ↘
B: *That's right. I'm from Santander.*

3 With positive statements, we usually use a negative question tag.

*I'm early, **aren't I**?   He's very friendly, **isn't he**?*

With negative statements, we usually use a positive question tag.

*It isn't difficult, **is it**?   She doesn't like dogs, **does she**?*

4 With *be*, modal verbs (*can, must, should, will, might*, etc.), *have got* and the present perfect, we repeat the auxiliary verb in the tag.

*They aren't from here, **are they**?*
*You'll come to my party, **won't you**?*
*We haven't got any milk, **have we**?*
*They've gone away on holiday, **haven't they**?*

5 With all other verbs, we use *do / don't / does / doesn't* (present simple) or *did / didn't* (past simple).

*You love this song, **don't you**?*
*I gave it back to you, **didn't I**?*

nor / neither / so do I

1 When someone says something and we want to agree with it, we can use *so / nor* (or *neither*) + auxiliary verb + *I*.

I am really happy.   **So am I.**
I don't like cold showers.   **Nor (Neither) do I.**

2 We use *so* to agree with a positive statement / idea, and *nor* (or *neither*) to agree with a negative statement or idea.

*I **was** tired yesterday.*   **So was I.**
*I **didn't enjoy** the film.*   **Nor (Neither) did I.**

3 Notice that the auxiliary we use after *so / nor / neither* depends on what the other person says.

*I **can't** sing.*   **Neither can I.**
*I**'ve been** to Paris.*   **So have I.**

UNIT 8
Past simple vs. past continuous (review)

1 When we talk about the past, we use the past simple for actions that happened at one particular time. We use the past continuous for background actions.

*When Steve **phoned** me, I **was reading** a book.*
*Who **scored** the goal? I **wasn't watching**.*

2 We often use *when* followed by the past simple, and *while* followed by the past continuous.

*She was swimming **when** the shark **attacked**.*
***While** I **was revising** for the test, I fell asleep.*

used to

1 We can use *used to* when we want to talk about an action which happened regularly in the past, but which doesn't happen any more.

*My mother **used to work** in a bank. (= My mother worked in a bank in the past, but she doesn't any more.)*

2 *used to* is followed by the base form of the main verb.

*Our team used to **be** much better than it is now.*

3 The negative of *used to* is *didn't use to*.

*I **didn't use to like** rap music. (= In the past I didn't like rap music, but now I like it.)*

We make questions with *used to* using *Did* + subject + *use to …?*

***Did** you **use to go** to school in Leeds?*

Second conditional

1 We use the second conditional to talk about unreal or imagined situations in the present or future.

*If I **was** good at tennis, I **would play** for the school team. (= I am not good at tennis, and don't play for the school team.)*
*She **wouldn't be** in the photography class if she **wasn't** interested in it. (= She is here because she is interested in it.)*

2 The second conditional has two parts (or 'clauses'). We usually make the second conditional like this:

If clause	Main clause
if + past simple +	comma *would/wouldn't* + main verb
If I **lived** in town,	I**'d go** to the cinema more often.
If he **was** nicer,	more people **would talk** to him.

We can change the order of the two clauses if we want to. When we put the *if* clause first, we write a comma (,) after it. If we put the main clause first, there is no comma.

*I **would go** to the cinema more often if I **lived** in town.*

3 The word *would* is often spoken as *'d*. We can write it like this in informal writing, too. Also *would not* is often spoken as *wouldn't*.

I wish

When we want to talk about how we would like something in the present to be different, we can use *I wish* + past tense.

*I wish you **were** here. (= You are not here and I am not happy about it.)*
*I wish we **could go** out tonight. (= We can not go out tonight and I am not happy about it.)*
*I wish it **wasn't** raining today. (= It is raining today and I am not happy about it.)*

UNIT 9

The passive (present simple, past simple, present continuous, present perfect)

1 We use the passive when it isn't important who does the action, or when we don't know who does it. The passive is also used when the action is more important than who does/did it.

*These cars **are made** in Japan. (It isn't important who makes them.)*
*This house **was built** in 1895. (We don't know who built it.)*

2 The passive is formed with the verb *be* + the past participle of a verb. The verb *be* can be in any tense.

Present simple passive:
*These watches **are sold** all over the world.*
Present continuous passive:
*I think **we are being watched**.*
Past simple passive:
*The city **was destroyed** in an earthquake.*
Present perfect passive:
*An important decision **has been taken** today.*

UNIT 10

Past perfect simple

1 We use the past perfect when we need to make it clear that one action happened *before* another action in the past.

*When we <u>got to</u> the theatre, the play **had started**.*
(= The play started before we got to the theatre.)

    Compare this with:
*When we <u>got to</u> the theatre, the play **started**.*
(= The play started when/after we got to the theatre.)

2 We form the past perfect with *had ('d)* / *had not (hadn't)* + the past participle of the main verb.

*She didn't watch the film because she **had seen** it.*

Past perfect continuous

1 We use the past perfect continuous to talk about situations or activities that started in the past and were still continuing at another time in the past.

*She was very tired because she **had been working** for a very long time.*
*When he got there, she **had been waiting** for an hour.*

2 We form the past perfect continuous with the past perfect of the verb *to be (had (not) been)* + the *-ing* form of the main verb.

*I didn't know the answer to the question because I **hadn't been listening**.*

3 The past perfect continuous focuses on how long an activity had been happening. It talks about situations or activities that may have stopped and may have had a result in the past.

*The ground was very wet because it **had been raining** all night.*
*We were tired because we**'d been travelling** since the day before.*

UNIT 11
Reported statements

1 When we report what someone said in the past, we use reported speech. In reported speech, we often use the verb *said* or *told (me)*.

    'The music's terrible,' my friend said. → *My friend **said** the music was terrible.*

2 We can use the word *that* between *said* or *told (me)* and the rest of the sentence, or we can leave it out.

    *I **said that** I wasn't hungry.* OR *I **said** I wasn't hungry.*

3 We often change the verb tense between direct speech and reported speech, like this:

Direct speech	Reported speech
Present (simple/continuous)	→ Past (simple/continuous)
Past (simple/continuous)	→ Past perfect (simple/continuous)
Present perfect	→ Past perfect
am/is/are going to	→ *was/were going to*
can/can't	→ *could/couldn't*
will/won't	→ *would/wouldn't*

Verb patterns

1 A common structure in English is verb + personal noun/pronoun + *to* infinitive.

    *I **want you to stay**.* (NOT: *I want that you stay.*)
    *He **asked Sarah to help** him.* (NOT: *He asked that Sarah helped him.*)

2 There are many verbs that follow this structure. (See Student's Book Unit 11 page 107)

    *He **told us to be** quiet.*
    *My parents **encouraged my brother to go** to university.*
    *They **warned us not to** go in.*
    *He **reminded the children not to be** late.*

UNIT 12
be allowed to / let

1 We use *be allowed to* to say that you do (or don't) have permission to do something. It is a passive construction: it is not important who gives (or doesn't give) the permission.

    *At my school, we **are allowed to** wear trainers.*
    *You **aren't allowed to** cycle here.*

2 We use *let* to say that someone gives you, or doesn't give you, permission to do something. It is an active construction.

    *I **let** my brother borrow my tablet sometimes.*
    *Our teacher **didn't let** us use dictionaries in the test.*

3 With *let*, the structure is *let* + person + infinitive without *to*.

    *She **didn't let me answer** the question.*
    *I'm not going to **let you borrow** my pen.*

4 With *be allowed to*, the structure is person + the correct form of *be* + *allowed* + *to* infinitive.

    *You **aren't allowed to leave** your bikes here.*

Third conditional

1 We use the third conditional to talk about unreal, imaginary situations in the past and their imagined results.

    If you had practised, you wouldn't have lost.
    (= You <u>didn't practise</u>, and you <u>lost</u>.)

2 The third conditional has two parts (or clauses). We usually make the third conditional like this:

if clause	Main clause
If + past perfect	*would have / wouldn't have* + main verb
If my sister **had asked** me	I**'d have told** her
If I**'d heard** the alarm clock,	I **wouldn't have been** late.

3 We can change the order of the two clauses if we want to.

    *I **would have told** my sister **if** she**'d asked** me.*
    *I **wouldn't have been** late **if** I**'d heard** the alarm clock.*

4 When we put the *if* clause first, we write a comma (,) after it. When we put the main clause first, there is no comma.

IRREGULAR VERBS

Base form	Past simple	Past participle
be	was / were	been
beat	beat	beaten
become	became	become
begin	began	begun
break	broke	broken
bring	brought	brought
build	built	built
buy	bought	bought
can	could	–
catch	caught	caught
choose	chose	chosen
come	came	come
cost	cost	cost
cut	cut	cut
do	did	done
draw	drew	drawn
drink	drank	drunk
drive	drove	driven
eat	ate	eaten
fall	fell	fallen
feel	felt	felt
fight	fought	fought
find	found	found
fly	flew	flown
forget	forgot	forgotten
get	got	got
give	gave	given
go	went	gone
grow	grew	grown
hang	hung	hung
have	had	had
hear	heard	heard
hit	hit	hit
hurt	hurt	hurt
hold	held	held
keep	kept	kept
know	knew	known
lead	led	led
leave	left	left
lend	lent	lent

Base form	Past simple	Past participle
let	let	let
lie	lay	lain
light	lit	lit
lose	lost	lost
make	made	made
mean	meant	meant
meet	met	met
pay	paid	paid
put	put	put
read / riːd/	read /red/	read /red/
ride	rode	ridden
ring	rang	rung
rise	rose	risen
run	ran	run
say	said	said
see	saw	seen
sell	sold	sold
send	sent	sent
set	set	set
shoot	shot	shot
show	showed	shown
sing	sang	sung
sit	sat	sat
sleep	slept	slept
speak	spoke	spoken
spend	spent	spent
stand	stood	stood
steal	stole	stolen
strike	struck	struck
swim	swam	swum
take	took	taken
teach	taught	taught
tell	told	told
think	thought	thought
throw	threw	thrown
understand	understood	understood
wake	woke	woken
wear	wore	worn
win	won	won
write	wrote	written